Law and Politics in Inter-American Diplomacy

Law and Politics in

John Wiley & Sons, Inc.

New York & London

Inter-American Diplomacy

C. Neale Ronning

Printed in the United States of America

Acknowledgments

I wish to thank especially Professor Edgar S. Furniss of Princeton University for his reading of the manuscript and for countless other considerations shown to me while this book was in preparation. For reading or other assistance I am also grateful to Professors Leon Gordenker, John B. Whitton, H. H. Wilson, and Harold Sprout of Princeton University, and to Mrs. R. C. Wilkinson of the *Princeton Packett*.

Much assistance in gathering data was offered by the library staff of the University of San Marcos in Lima, Peru and by Dr. Manuel G. Abastos of the Faculty of Law. *The Journal of Inter-American Studies* gave permission to reprint portions of an article by the author which appeared in that journal. The Columbia University Press and *International Affairs* (London) have given permission to reproduce maps.

C. NEALE RONNING

New Orleans
April, 1963

Contents

Chapter One

Introduction

The vision of an America regulated by its own unique legal order arose with the achievement of independence. It has inspired, amused, interested and frustrated countless writers and statesmen ever since. Rudimentary bits and pieces of such a legal order soon began to develop as the states in this hemisphere set out to formalize various aspects of their mutual relations. By the middle of the present century a substantial but uncoordinated and confusing pattern had emerged.

In 1948, the American states* met at Bogotá to consolidate, formalize and improve many of the institutions which had developed in this rather haphazard manner. Shortly after the conference the Mexican Minister of Foreign Affairs offered a timely summary and prediction: "After more than a century of exploration, of uncertainties and of trials, the legal channels of Panamericanism have been decisively consolidated. What currents will flow in these channels? America will say."[1]

A decade later one could only say that those currents were rough, muddy and of uncertain direction. United States military and other assistance offered to Cuban exiles in open contradiction to conventional obligations has been only the most dramatic expression of an increasing tendency throughout the Western Hemisphere openly to disregard formerly accepted legal obligations when political expedi-

* Throughout this study, references to "the American states" or "all the American states" should be understood as excluding Canada. Thus, these references refer to the United States plus the twenty Latin American republics.

ency so requires. Foreign fishing vessels have been seized by South American governments well over a hundred miles from their shore— in waters traditionally regarded as high seas. The confiscation of billions of dollars worth of foreign-owned property is viewed by many as only a tardy arrival of justice. To others it is the crumbling of the last vestiges of order and stability.

Obviously this is not a new phenomenon. Wherever and whenever we observe the relations among states, two conflicting desires are evident: the desire for order and predictability on the one hand, and the desire for freedom of action on the other. The former would seek a maximum mutual subjection to a minimum set of rules of conduct; the latter would seek a minimum of subjection to them.

In contemporary inter-American affairs there can be no escaping the fact that emphasis is now on freedom of action. It is true, of course, that much sentimental nonsense has been written about the extent to which inter-American relations have been governed by legal norms, in contrast to the evils of power and politics in other parts of the world. Yet, when all this has been relegated to its proper place, the fact remains that many of the important aspects of the relations among American states have for the most part conformed to commonly accepted rules. Many of the conflicts now troubling this hemisphere serve to remind us of the usefulness of a number of rules and practices once taken for granted. More rules, once generally accepted as obligatory, are now being questioned, ignored or given totally new interpretations by more American states than ever before.

Those who would guard the *status quo* will feel that we have fallen upon evil days and are confronted by evil men. But the American, French and Mexican Revolutions, all of them challenges to law and order, will surely deny us this easy conclusion. The solution to this difficult state of affairs will not be found in more painstaking efforts to show, on the basis of traditional sources of international law, what the rules are that states are bound to observe. Nor will it be found in moral remonstrances and logical arguments, however learned, giving the advantages of an effective legal order. There would certainly be wide agreement on this if the question "what kind of a legal order?" or "whose legal order?" could be answered first.

We must begin by learning what we can about the economic, political and social forces which are producing these profound changes in attitudes toward so many of the traditional rules. We must also learn what we can about the economic, political and social forces which formed the sphere of application and conditioned the effectiveness of rules which at times were reasonably effective. In short we must confront the task outlined by Charles de Visscher—"one of submitting to a more realistically informed criticism the rules and practices of international law observed in their living application, and of identifying the political, economic and demographic factors that shape, sustain, and develop them, as well as those that help to distort or destroy them."[2]

The chapters that follow will show some of the complex forces which at times produce an emphasis on the desire for order and predictability, at other times an emphasis on the desire for freedom of action. We shall examine in detail some of the more crucial and some not-so-crucial inter-American questions which are currently the subject of conflicting legal interpretations. We shall see how the recognition of governments, perhaps the most fundamental question in international intercourse, has been governed by two conflicting doctrines, each of which shows the stamp of economic, social and political forces which refuse to stand still. The treatment of aliens and the expropriation of their property, the doctrines of non-intervention, the control of coastal waters and the ownership of the Antarctic are some of the other questions that will be studied. For each the economic, political and social forces which condition the changing doctrines and legal interpretations will be the central theme. These complex forces are revealed in four phenomena which confront us at every turn: cold war, social revolution, anticolonialism and nationalism.

In many ways the inter-American system is particularly well suited to this kind of study. In no area of the world has there been so much discussion and serious effort directed toward the formation of a regional legal order. These efforts have produced a jungle of "organizations" and periodic meetings. Some have been abolished, some replaced, some duplicated and some simply forgotten.

There are, first of all, the general, Inter-American Conferences normally attended by all American states, with the respective ministers of foreign affairs heading the delegations. The conferences have convened roughly every five years since the first one was convened at Washington in 1889. Before the Tenth Conference they were called International Conferences of American States, but both names have long been used in official literature as well as unofficial. Resolutions have been passed and conventions have been signed relating to almost any matter of inter-American interest. More than one hundred multilateral conventions have been signed; a few have been ratified by all states, many by a large majority and others by very few or none. These conventions and resolutions are referred to in countless diplomatic exchanges, where they are used as a means of showing what the majority feeling is on a particular question.

Whether or not conventions are ratified, or even signed, the conferences have provided an arena where Latin American states have been able on a number of occasions to demonstrate a solidarity of opinion—a gauge of what has been considered just or unjust and, thus, a measure of the limits within which a state (especially the United States) can act if it wishes to avoid widespread antagonism throughout Latin America.

The Council of the Organization of American States (with representatives from all the American states), which sits in permanent session in Washington, tends to fulfill this same function, although to a much lesser extent. In addition, there are the irregular Meetings of Consultation of the Ministers of Foreign Affairs, convened as the need arises.

The idea of a specialized body to assist the conferences in elaborating codes of public and private international law was considered as early as the Second International Conference of American States held at Mexico City in 1901–1902. Here a convention was signed which contemplated the establishment of an International Commission of Jurists, but since it did not receive the required number of ratifications, nothing ever came of it. A similar convention, signed at the following conference, had a better fate, and in 1912 the Commission of Jurists convened with sixteen states represented. The work of this meeting was confined almost entirely to organization and procedure, but the Commission also formed six subcommittees which would be located in different capitals with each devoting itself to one specific problem of codification.

A second meeting of the International Commission of Jurists was to have been held in 1914, but because of World War I and other reasons (they are always legion in inter-American affairs) it was postponed until 1927. At this meeting the Commission considered and approved a number of projects, which were eventually submitted to the Sixth International Conference of American States in 1928. Some of the most important conventions in inter-American affairs came out of these projects—conventions on asylum, Diplomatic Agents, Consular Agents, Rights and Duties of States in Time of Civil Strife, Maritime Neutrality, Status of Aliens, and the Bustamante Code of Private International Law.

During the two decades following 1928, various juridical committees were added and abolished in an uncertain and confusing relationship to one another. By 1948 it was decided that the machinery for codification was badly in need of revision and simplification. At this time the Inter-American Council of Jurists was created as the central agency responsible for codification. The Council is composed of representatives of all the members of the Organization of American States and meets every two or three years in different American capitals. It has a permanent committee, a continuing body of nine legal experts, from nine countries selected by the Inter-American Conference. This committee, called the Inter-American Juridical Committee, is actually the continuation of a committee with the same name which has functioned since 1942.

Studies and projects prepared by the Inter-American Juridical Committee are submitted to the Council of Jurists or to other inter-American bodies which may have requested them. Even those that are never approved as inter-American conventions or resolutions find their way into diplomatic exchanges and international meetings to demonstrate support for a particular legal position.

The desire to bring order and predictability into inter-American relations has been the progenitor of this assortment of "organizations." Efforts directed toward this end, their successes and failures, have taken place within a complex of economic, political and social forces. The preservation of a measure of order and predictability in the immediate future will be no less complicated. The following pages will attempt to trace some of the relationships between these evolving forces and the rules or practices that are applied in the relations among American states. Patterns of law and politics which emerge from this will be sketched in the final chapter.

FOOTNOTES

1. Jaime Torres Bodet, "Transformación del panamericanismo," *Inter-American Juridical Yearbook*, 1948 (Washington, D.C., 1949), p. 69.
2. *Theory and Reality in Public International Law*, trans. by P. E. Corbett (Princeton, 1957), p. 364.

Chapter Two

Law, Politics and the
Recognition of Governments

Politics and recognition

Formal diplomatic intercourse represents only a part of the whole pattern of international relations. Yet all other forms of intercourse are vitally affected by these formal relations. Commercial, cultural and even political relations may be carried on, but inevitably they are restricted by the absence of diplomatic ties. In the Western Hemisphere, where the influence of the United States has been so preponderant, the existence of formal relations has been of particular importance. A Latin American government which had no diplomatic relations with the United States soon found its other channels of intercourse seriously threatened.

The various acts by which governments make known their intentions to maintain normal diplomatic relations with other governments are referred to, in the language of diplomacy, as "recognition." In more precise terminology, this would be "recognition of governments" as distinguished from "recognition of states," but since we will be concerned only with the former, the distinction need not concern us here.

It is the purpose of this chapter to show the relationship between national and domestic (private) interests of a given era and the emergence and application of two opposing doctrines related to the recognition of governments. One, which we shall call the American Doctrine,[1] calls for the recognition of governments whenever they fulfill certain fairly objective requirements—*de facto* control of the state and ability (sometimes "willingness" is added) to discharge international obligations. The other, which we shall call the Doctrine of Legitimacy,[2] adds certain more subjective requirements—dynastic legitimacy, monarchical legitimacy, constitutional legitimacy, ideological legitimacy, and so forth.

During certain periods a particular combination of circumstances has moved the great majority of governments to take this important aspect of international relations out of the realm of politics. At such times the doctrine that calls for recognition of a new government upon fulfillment of the fairly objective criteria just mentioned receives almost universal application. Practice during such periods has often led to the assumption that recognition is regarded by states as a legal act and that governments have a right to be recognized and a corresponding duty to extend recognition.

During other periods the national interest or powerful domestic interests of a number of states have made it impossible to apply the American Doctrine. During these periods the primacy of those interests can be seen in the additional prerequisites which are added to the fairly objective requirements we have pointed to. The Doctrine of Legitimacy, once an instrument of the Concert of Europe and a prop of the balance of power system, assumed that what happened within national societies was very much a matter of concern to the Great Powers. But the doctrine could be an effective instrument only as long as they agreed upon this, as long as they agreed upon the consequences of certain of these domestic events and as long as they were willing to take action accordingly. It did indeed provide an important element of stability for the balance of power system, which required a number of strong and independent units. The American Revolution, the French Revolution and, later, events in South America led the rulers of Europe to the true realization of the consequences of a failure to respect the "sanctity" of "legitimate" governments. Thus the test of legitimacy loomed large at the Congress of Vienna. But the doctrine received its most explicit statement only after the international order which had brought it into being, and which it was intended to perpetuate, was seriously threatened by the relentless forces of change. With the passing of the Holy Alliance the doctrine of legitimacy also passed from the scene.[3] Forces of change in the world rendered the old principle inadequate to meet the needs of an emerging order.

The emergence of the American Doctrine

The essence of the American Doctrine of Recognition was expressed in Jefferson's instructions concerning the policy that the United States would follow with regard to revolutionary France.

We certainly cannot deny to other nations that principle upon which our government is founded, that every nation has a right to govern itself internally under what form it pleases and to change these forms at its own will; and externally to transact business with other nations through whatever organ it chooses whether that be King, Convention, Assembly, Committee or President or whatever it be. The only thing essential is the will of the nation.[4]

As an outgrowth of the idea of popular sovereignty and the right of revolution, the doctrine clearly bears the imprint of Jefferson's political thinking. As an expression of ideas widely accepted throughout the New World, the doctrine received the enthusiastic endorsement of other new states in this hemisphere. There was, of course, little doubt that the new governments would be willing to deal with monarchies. They could refuse to do so only at the expense of isolating themselves from the important states of the world. Thus the American Doctrine was especially practical at this time, for it provided the grounds for avoiding an impossible situation which might have been demanded by revolutionary zeal. At the same time, it implicitly stated the case for recognition of the new republics.

But what of the Great Powers of Europe? Technically, of course, their problem was first presented as one of recognition of new states, but for purposes of our discussion the principles involved remain the same.

Britain's policy is of particular interest, inasmuch as it shows very clearly that government's understanding of the requirements of an emerging international order and of the necessity to adjust its policy to these changes. Shortly after British recognition had been extended to some of the new Latin American republics, George Canning (himself predisposed to monarchy) pointed out why it had been necessary to do so. In a letter to a close friend, he emphasized the requirements of British security and, indeed, the security of all of Europe.

The thing is done. . . . The Yankees will shout in triumph; but it is they who will lose most by our decision. The great danger of our time—a danger which the policy of the European system would have fostered, was a division of the world into European and American, Republican and Monarchical; a league of worn out Governments on the one hand, and of youthful and stirring Nations, with the United States at their head, on the other. . . . The United States have gotten the start on us in vain; and we will link once more America to Europe. Six months more—and the mischief would have been done.[5]

Once Britain had adopted such a policy, other Great Powers of Europe were forced to follow suit or forgo the advantages that regular diplomatic relations offered.[6]

The American Doctrine also met the needs of important domestic interests both in Britain and the United States. Uninterrupted and amicable political relations were essential for continued expansion of private trade and investment activities. The history of United States investment in Latin America began before 1830, especially in Mexico, Cuba and Chile. By 1870 there was hardly a Latin American country which United States investors had not reached.[7] The American Doctrine was particularly well suited to fill these needs in view of the unstable political conditions in the area. In this unstable and turbulent political environment, it avoided the dangerous choice between rival factions. Since it was a policy strongly advocated by Latin Americans themselves,[8] the United States was not as a rule condemned by opposition groups for its relations with the regime in power.

This relatively detached attitude was possible only in the absence of irreconcilable economic and social issues which would later bring new bitterness into the domestic struggles of Latin America. Most of the nineteenth-century political struggles were contests within a small oligarchy or among a few military figures. As such they affected few people and scarcely involved questions of deep economic or social significance. Even movements that proclaimed "democracy" as their goal usually reached only a small minority of wealthy and educated people. They were extremely moderate, and repercussions, as far as international relations were concerned, were insignificant. The regularity with which the American Doctrine could be applied was due to the fact that it proved mutually advantageous to powerful domestic interests and to the national interests of states throughout the hemisphere.

The first challenge to the American Doctrine

Ironically enough, it was the continued expansion of United States private investments throughout Latin America and a corresponding increase in European investments that were behind the first challenge to the American Doctrine. Latin American countries of course needed foreign capital and welcomed it from both sources. By 1897 nearly one-half of about $700 million in United States foreign investments had gone into the lands where Cortes, Pizarro, Quesada and others had sought much the same "El Dorado." By the end of 1914 this figure had exceeded $1.6 billion—about 46 percent of the total of United States foreign investment.[9]

But real and imagined abuses inflicted by foreign creditors caused growing resentment and hostility. This situation, plus the chronic financial difficulties in which Latin American governments found themselves, were the ingredients for increasing trouble over the honoring of contracts. Creditors sought the assistance of their governments, and actual or threatened intervention by European states and by the United States soon followed.

The problem of United States security became involved. By the turn of the century the United States was moving into a position as a world power and, as such, our government became more and more concerned over events in Central America and the Caribbean. The vigorous nationalism of the new generation which had grown to manhood since the grim day at Appomattox provided an explosive element in this new situation. More than ever before, United States policy makers began to think in terms of the need to control this area, or at least to keep it out of European hands. The domestic affairs of Latin American countries thus became a matter of United States concern.

Continued and uninterrupted diplomatic relations with Latin American states were still important. But the *kind* of government now assumed a new importance, and measures were taken to make sure that new governments would have the proper attitude toward investments. Non-recognition was one of the milder pressures that could be used.

Thus, by the end of the nineteenth century, United States recognition policy had begun to emphasize the ability of new governments to carry out the international obligations of the state.[10] After the turn of the century the trend became even more pronounced, emphasizing both the ability and the *willingness* of a new government to fulfill the commitments of previous regimes to foreign governments and nationals.[11] "It now became a specific prerequisite and recognition was often refused on this basis."[12] More important, precise and detailed agreements were now required instead of the previous general commitments to fulfill international obligations. Prior agreements to ac-

cept arbitration of specific claims or a prior agreement which itself settled specific claims often replaced the previous general stipulations.[13]
Whether this was the result of conditioned thinking on the part of
policy makers or direct pressure from interests affected need not concern us here. In either event, it was a clear demonstration of the
connection between economic interests and recognition policy.

Under the Wilson administration an additional dimension was added
to our recognition policy. It is important to note the main features
of this policy and the forces behind it, because it had elements of the
same reforming zeal which would later contribute to an about-face in
the recognition policies of a number of Latin American states. It was
to have a brief day in Argentine policy of this same period. When
it returned in a modified form in the policies of other Latin American
states, it was to shake the foundation of a practice long defended as
a rule of law by most of these governments.

The reforming zeal which we refer to here was apparent in Wilson's First Inaugural Address.

We hold, as I am sure all thoughtful leaders of republican government
everywhere hold, that just government rests always upon the consent of
the governed, and there can be no freedom without order based upon law
and upon public conscience and approval. We shall look to make these
principles the basis of mutual intercourse, respect and helpfulness between
our sister republics and ourselves.[14]

As Wilson's "New Freedom" recognized the need of positive action
to promote the freedoms that Jefferson had thought would be insured
by stringent limitations upon government, so did Wilson's recognition
policy imply a need for positive action in the international sphere to
promote the form of government that Jefferson had been certain
would "roll round the globe."[15] Both of these twentieth-century attitudes would be present in much stronger form in the Latin American
movements to be discussed.

Thus to the existing policy, which demanded respect for property
and for other international obligations, Wilson added his requirement
of constitutionalism. In order to receive our recognition a new government must have come into power by constitutional means and
must represent the will of the people.[16] Although his doctrine was
not without important economic overtones,[17] the emphasis was clearly
on morality rather than economic interests.

With the advent of the Harding administration the Wilsonian doctrine was largely, though not entirely, abandoned, but the requirement

that contractual obligations be honored continued to be applied.[18] It would be another decade before the United States returned to a practice much closer to the nineteenth-century American Doctrine. Then, in the decade following 1933, an equilibrium was reestablished which made possible, once again, the application of the American Doctrine. The forces responsible for this must now occupy our attention.

Latin American reactions: the American Doctrine reinstated

Although there were exceptions, the overwhelming majority of Latin American jurists and governments continued to support the American Doctrine of Recognition. There was, therefore, widespread opposition to United States policies which, contrary to the doctrine, insisted on the prerequisites just discussed. Most vociferous of all was the opposition to the practice that made recognition dependent on the acceptance by a new government of certain agreements to protect private foreign interests.[19] This opposition found increased expression in both private and official efforts.

At the request of the Pan American Union, the American Institute of International Law prepared a number of projects to be submitted to the 1927 meeting of the International Commission of American Jurists. One of these projects provided that "every abnormally constituted government may be recognized if it is capable of maintaining order and tranquility and is disposed to fulfill the international obligations of the nation."[20] Although this project clearly made recognition permissive (as far as "abnormally constituted" governments were concerned), the changes which the International Commission of American Jurists wrote into this project clearly made recognition a legal obligation. Article 8 of the Commission's final version provided that

A Government is to be recognized whenever it fulfills the following conditions:
1. Effective authority with a probability of stability and consolidation . . .
2. Capacity to discharge preexisting international obligations, to contract others and to respect the principles established by international law.[21]

Three features stand out here: (1) recognition is made obligatory provided that certain fairly objective criteria are fulfilled, (2) *capacity*, not *willingness*, to fulfill international obligations is explicitly indicated, and (3) nothing is said regarding the method by which a government has been constituted.

When the project was circulated to member governments, the United States offered the objection that it had not included "willingness," as well as "capacity," to discharge international obligations.[22] Eventually the project came before the Sixth International Conference of American States, but discussion on these particular points seems to have been left aside in the bitter debate over a more controversial article which clearly outlawed intervention by one state in the internal affairs of another. United States opposition to this latter article was sufficient to postpone action on the entire project. The article on intervention was, however, only a more inclusive reference to a number of United States policies, including that of non-recognition. There had never been much doubt that Latin Americans regarded this as a form of intervention, and the sharpest debates that had ever taken place at an inter-American conference left no doubt about Latin American attitudes toward United States policies of the past quarter century.[23]

Mexico's experience with United States recognition policies, and her violent opposition to them, led to the pronouncement of the Estrada Doctrine in 1930. President Wilson's long delay in recognizing the Caranza regime and, after Caranza's assassination, the recognition of the Obregon government only after the signing of the Bucareli Agreements were particularly objectionable memories to Mexicans. The Bucareli Agreements provided machinery for adjustment of claims by nationals of one country against the other. Mexico also gave informal assurance of a loose definition of the positive acts necessary for validation of mineral concessions and promised to issue agrarian bonds or pay cash for expropriated properties depending on the size of the properties.[24] Secretary Estrada declared that the future policy of Mexico regarding new governments would be that of

. . . issuing no declarations in the sense of grants of recognition, since that nation considers that such a course is an insulting practice and one which, in addition to the fact that it offends the sovereignty of other nations, implies that judgment of some sort may be placed upon the internal affairs of those nations by other governments. . . .[25]

The wide acclaim with which this doctrine was received throughout Latin America was significant more as an indication of general resentment toward the United States than as an indication of policies that Latin American governments had practiced or would practice. Nor has Mexico herself consistently followed such a policy. But it left no doubt concerning the adverse feeling that United States recognition policies had earned among articulate and influential groups in Latin America.[26]

Although the Hoover administration took some steps in the direction of quieting Latin American fear of intervention, the need to make this a cornerstone of United States policy was more clearly recognized and acted upon by the administration of Franklin Roosevelt. The fact that by 1933 finance capitalism had become more widely discredited than ever before in the United States made it politically easier for the new administration to make distinctions between the national interest and support for private interests in Latin America. The growing power of Nazism and Fascism on the European continent, though not at first regarded as a threat to the United States, later contributed to the realization that it would be necessary to improve our relations within the hemisphere.[27] The *Memoirs* of Cordell Hull show that even as early as 1933 the threat of a darkening world situation and the consequent need to repair our relations with Latin America were matters of concern to him on the eve of his departure for the Montevideo Conference at the end of that year.[28] "Over a long period until almost 1933," he observed, "The United States had pursued policies towards some Latin American nations of so arbitrary—and what some of these countries considered to be so overbearing—a nature that prejudice and feeling throughout Central and South America against our country were sharp indeed."[29]

Thus, with the initiation of Franklin Roosevelt's Good Neighbor Policy, we returned to something much closer to the American Doctrine of the nineteenth century. Although we generally dropped the practice of insisting upon *written* assurances that the new government would honor its international obligations, oral assurances were sometimes required and a phrase noting that such assurance had been given was often included in our note extending recognition. But a statement of willingness to honor "international obligations" was something quite different from the more specific assurances that previous administrations had demanded. A declaration of willingness to honor international obligations was, after all, open to various interpretations, and Latin American states have also insisted on such assurances from one another.[30]

The following case is typical. In May 1936, our Department of State faced the problem of recognition of a military *junta* in Bolivia which had declared the need to strengthen the nation's economy "within purely socialistic standards."[31] Some concern was expressed but the Department was willing to settle for only a very general assurance.[32] Ten days after the regime had come to power recognition was extended.[33] The Bolivian Minister of Foreign Affairs had indeed given assurances that his government intended "to respect its international obligations," and it was "in view of this affirmation" that recognition was extended.[34]

Early in the following year the Bolivian government did in fact move against the Standard Oil Company, expropriating the entire property of the company and transfering it to the state.[35] In July the military *junta* resigned, turning the reins of government over to a provisional president but leaving the question of Standard Oil properties still unresolved. Discussions continued while the question of recognition was pending, but settlement was not made a condition for recognition. About a week later our Ambassador to Argentina reported the results of his discussion with the Bolivian Minister of Foreign Affairs.

Standard Oil Company confiscation was discussed at length and both incoming Ministers agreed to the recommendations which I made in a purely personal capacity, viz: (1) that the matter be referred to a committee of reputable citizens in order to at least tide over the present strong public opinion favoring confiscation, (2) to encourage foreign capital investment Bolivia must make some deal with Standard Oil Company perhaps along the lines followed by Chile with the American Foreign Power Company.[36]

Three days later our *chargé d'affaires* in Bolivia was instructed to extend recognition in view "of the declarations made by the Chief Executive that his Government intends to respect Bolivia's international obligations and the legitimate rights of private property."[37]

In most instances it became fairly standard practice for a new government to state on its own initiative that it intended to "honor its international obligations" or "abide by the obligations of general international law," and such a statement was accepted as adequate by our government. Although we did not, strictly speaking, return to a policy which simply *assumed* that a new government would honor its international obligations, we did, nevertheless, follow a policy far removed from that of the first three decades of this century. For more than a decade it was again possible to bring this aspect of inter-American relations out of the realm of political considerations. But no sooner was this precarious equilibrium reestablished than new forces emerged which again brought the question of recognition back into the realm of domestic and international politics.

The challenge of social revolution

Contemporary social movements in Latin America are having a profound effect on the recognition policies of many of the states in the area. Today's struggles seek fundamental changes in the entire social structure and concern far more people than did the numerous political disturbances of the previous century.

The election of Hipólito Irigoyen in Argentina (1916) provides an interesting introduction to this aspect of our study. This election was not, to be sure, the result of an economic and social movement of the type that began to emerge in the 1930's. But it was, nevertheless, an event that had a tremendous emotional impact on a multitude of Argentines. Although Irigoyen came to power by only a narrow margin, his election was a great victory. It marked the emergence of the middle sectors in Argentine life. More important, it represented the culmination of a long struggle by the Radical party for electoral reform and political democracy. As such it brought into office a new group of men who had hitherto been excluded from political life.[38] In this sense, the triumph of Irigoyen brought with it some of the zeal that would be so important an element in the social and economic movements destined to appear later.

The recognition policy of the Irigoyen government bore the imprint of these popular emotions. In 1920, its policy was explained with regard to the newly created states in Europe. The Argentine government would, according to the announcement, proceed to recognize them whenever they appeared as an expression of democratic ideals.[39] That same year recognition was refused to a Bolivian government which had come to power by revolution. Recognition would be withheld until a government elected by a popular majority in accordance with the constitution was in power.[40]

But mass movements were still a long way off in Latin America. When they emerged in the 1930's, the emphasis was on freeing the oppressed masses from four centuries of economic and social bondage. But the full impact of these movements was not felt for more than a decade. World War II, with allied condemnation of dictatorship and promises of freedom and well-being for all mankind, provided a catalyst. The cold war, which followed almost immediately, furthered this process with a barrage of propaganda attempting to show all spectators how abundant life could be if only they would be careful to adopt the right system.

When a government depends on the support of "recently liberated" masses the messianic spirit that has put a new regime in power tends to extend into international relations. The leaders of a movement which has just overthrown a hated dictotorial regime with promises to sweep away the old order of poverty and inequality quite naturally appeal to their supporters by declaring their intention *not* to carry on relations with remaining dictators. A plea to other governments to isolate such regimes diplomatically usually follows.

The first manifestation of this came in Guatemala in 1944 with the overthrow of the brutal dictatorship of General Ubico. A presidential election was held late that year in which Dr. Juan José Arévalo won by an overwhelming vote.[41] His vague program, which he called "spiritual socialism," reflected both the zeal of popular opinion and the uncertainty and lack of experience of the new leadership: "Guatemala has stopped being a masquerade in order to convert itself into a democracy. . . . Now we are going to install a period of sympathy for the man who works in the fields, in the factories, the shops and in commerce."[42]

The program of the revolution was immediately reflected in Guatemala's attitude toward the question of recognition. At the Inter-American Conference on Problems of War and Peace, held at Mexico City early in 1945, Guatemala submitted a project for convention which asked the conference

1. To recommend to the American republics that they abstain from recognizing and maintaining relations with anti-democratic regimes which in the future might be established in any of the countries of the continent and, especially, with regimes which might come to power through a *coup d'état* against democratic governments legitimately constituted.
2. To recommend as a specific rule for judging such regimes, the extent to which the popular will of the respective country may have contributed to its establishment according to the judgment of each state.[43]

Although the project was not approved by the conference, Guatemala did in fact apply it in her own policy. In June 1947, the Foreign Ministry announced that it would not recognize the government which had been set up by force in neighboring Nicaragua.[44] A few days later President Arévalo ordered the suspension of diplomatic relations with the Dominican Republic: "While we should not meddle in the internal affairs of other countries no matter how grave they may be, we cannot be forced to maintain friendship with governments that have transformed republican practices into those of monarchy."[45] By the end of the year the Ministry noted that Costa Rica had recognized the Nicaraguan government but that Guatemala's policy was unchanged toward a government "opposed to the cherished democratic hopes of the Nicaraguan people."[46] In January of the following year it was announced that Guatemala was canceling even her recognition of the Dominican consul general, thus seemingly breaking off all relations.[47]

In Venezuela the fall of the tyrant, Gómez, in 1935, permitted at least some development of political parties during the following decade. The strongest of these, *Acción Democrática*, fired the imagination and gained the loyalty of a large part of the laboring people, middle class and peasantry of Venezuela. In 1945, Rómulo Betancourt as head of *Acción Democrática* was installed as Provisional President and Venezuela was to have her first experiment with democratic government and social-economic reform. The government's recognition policy shows the impact of such a movement. The report of the Ministry of Foreign Affairs for 1946–1947 is very clear on this point: "The Chancellery abstained from contacting regimes which held power in Spain and the Dominican Republic since it considered it improper (*improcedente*) for the recently constituted Revolutionary Government to enter into diplomatic relations with governments whose authority is not backed by the democratic opinion of majorities."[48]

With the "Revolutionary Government" overthrown and a military *junta* back in power, the report for 1948–1952 informs us that relations had been resumed with Spain, the Dominican Republic and Nicaragua. Equally significant is the fact that the governments of Costa Rica, Guatemala and Uruguay are missing from the list of countries with which diplomatic relations had been maintained. Needless to say, these three governments had been among the most outspoken against dictatorship.[49]

Policies shifted once again with the overthrow of the Pérez Jiménez regime in January 1958, but the precarious nature of the new coalition government was reflected in a less clearcut policy. In August 1959, the Minister of Foreign Affairs stated that his government would oppose any O.A.S. resolutions that invoked the agreements made at the Caracas Conference of 1954. This meeting, he said, held under the dictatorship of Marcos Pérez Jiménez, was a black blot on the history of the

O.A.S.[50] The implication would seem to be that the other American states should not have engaged in full diplomatic relations with this government. The following year Betancourt publicly urged the United States to follow his government's course and break off relations with the Trujillo dictatorship in the Dominican Republic.[51]

The impact of contemporary economic and social movements on recognition policies is vividly demonstrated by an episode in Bolivian politics in 1948. This was a period of intense agitation by labor groups and the outlawed M.N.R. (*Movimiento Nacionalista Revolucionario*) which would eventually triumph in the 1952 National Revolution. Although the government in power at this time was by no means a popular government, it did at least try to gain a measure of popular support through a coalition cabinet of center groups and some expression of criticism was permitted in the press. On the initiative of the Minister of Foreign Affairs, Paz Campero, Bolivia had been the first to recognize the military *junta* that came to power in Peru in 1948.[52] When a similar coup overthrew the constitutional government of Venezuela that same year, Paz Campero again favored recognition. Strong opposition in the majority of the press and from a number of cabinet ministers resulted in a deadlock within the government. Eventually, the Minister of Foreign Affairs resigned after three meetings had failed to bring about an agreement.[53] After his resignation Paz Campero went to Venezuela where he was decorated for his efforts by the Pérez government.[54] When a similar recognition problem faced the Bolivian government, following a *coup d'état* in Paraguay about two months later, his successor announced that Bolivia would not extend recognition.[55]

Pressure from leftist and reform groups rather than strong conviction on the part of governments probably accounts for occasional instances of similar policies in other Latin American countries. When Nicaraguan strong man, Somoza, removed the President whom he had permitted to be elected in 1946 (the President had shown an unexpected independence), there were mild objections from other Central American governments. The Foreign Minister of Panama announced that his government would not recognize the new regime that Somoza had placed in power.[56] The Foreign Ministry of El Salvador was quoted as saying that "it was not inclined to recognize the *de facto* government established in Nicaragua last week by a *coup d'état*."[57] Both El Salvador and Panama had for some time been plagued with troublesome but unsuccessful movements to bring an end to the old system of military oligarchies.[58] The limited success of the movement in El Salvador would soon present new recognition problems for other American states.[59]

After the overthrow of Batista in Cuba, the Castro government joined the ranks of those using recognition as an instrument of policy. The Cuban note breaking relations with the Dominican Republic asserted that "by reason of democratic standards and elemental principles of justice, by reason of our moral obligation with all the people of America and especially with the Dominican people, we cannot continue to maintain diplomatic relations with a government which in our opinion has violated all these principles."[60]

After reestablishment of relations with Guatemala, the Cuban Minister of Foreign Affairs took pains to point out the political significance of the act. He was, according to an official Guatemalan publication, "pleased with the moral support which the sending [of a minister] by Guatemala signifies for the Revolutionary Government of Cuba."[61]

Castro's announcement of non-recognition of the Rio Pact of 1947, since it was signed by the Batista government,[62] is of the same nature as the Venezuelan announcement about measures agreed upon at Caracas in 1954. Both would seem to imply that only obligations contracted by popularly supported governments need be honored. This would mean that other governments have to take into account the nature of *de facto* regimes with which they intend to deal.

The radical turn which the Castro government has taken has caused concern among a number of conservative though democratically inclined governments in Latin America. The impact of this fact became apparent in connection with the question of recognizing the government which came to power by *coup d'etat* in El Salvador on October 26, 1960. *The New York Times* reported that "Brazil and several South American Governments were reported . . . to have decided to continue to delay recognition of the ruling junta in El Salvador. They were said to have acted in light of indications that the new regime may have 'Cuban-type tendencies.' "[63] It is of course the appeal of the Castro movement and its reported subversive activities among dissatisfied groups in many Latin American countries which concerns these governments. By June 1961, seven Latin American governments had broken relations with Cuba, the Dominican Republic, Haiti, El Salvador, Honduras, Guatemala, Nicaragua and Peru.[64,*]

* When Argentina recalled its ambassador early in 1962, responding to strong pressure from the armed forces, only five Latin American states (Bolivia, Brazil, Chile, Haiti and Mexico) continued formal diplomatic relations with Cuba.

The challenge of cold war politics

The emergence of movements based on totalitarian ideologies and attempts to extend their influence into this hemisphere have added further complexities to the problem of recognition. German activities in this hemisphere during World War II first called attention to the problem of relations with *de facto* governments suspected of having close ties or sympathies with Nazi Germany.

At the Third Consultative Meeting of Foreign Ministers held at Rio de Janeiro, January 1942, an Emergency Consultative Committee for Political Defense was set up in order to combat subversive activities in the Americas by non-American states.[65] Whatever the original purpose of this Committee, the United States soon availed itself of its services to "consult" on the recognition of *de facto* governments where there might be suspicion of Nazi influence in a *coup d'état*.[66] Two relevant cases have been discussed elsewhere and will only be mentioned here.[67] The machinery was first used by the United States in order to delay recognition of the Villarroel government in Bolivia (December 1943) until it was satisfied about the future international policies of the latter.[68] Then, when the Farell government came to power in Argentina in February 1944, the United States was opposed to a proposal that an inter-American meeting be called to resolve the question of Argentine relations. Since a number of Latin American states had already extended recognition, there certainly would have been open disagreement at any such meeting. After more than a year (in April 1945), the United States finally extended formal recognition.[69] Neither experiment with non-recognition yielded very gratifying results. The complexion of the government in question remained unchanged in both instances, and the lack of agreement among the American states was only emphasized.

Two aspects of this wartime experience should be emphasized. First, when political expediency directed that the American Doctrine of Recognition would no longer fill the needs of our foreign policy, we did not hesitate to return to a policy of using non-recognition as a political instrument. But it is significant that we considered it unwise to return to a policy of *unilateral* non-recognition, even though the policy of "consultation" may have been largely a cloak of respectability. Second, and more important, the United States felt impelled to make it clear that this was a wartime measure and, as such, a matter of

determining who is the enemy in time of war. "The American Republics have expressly dictated," announced the Department of State, "that
this policy does not affect and has nothing to do with the ordinary
rules and procedure for recognition in time of peace."[70] On April 19,
1946, Secretary of State Byrnes announced that the United States
would resume its traditional recognition policy. In the future, recognition would be granted to all *de facto* governments, although this recognition should not be interpreted as implying approval of the politics
of these governments.[71]

The cold war policy of the Soviet Union presents the same type
of problem as that presented by Nazi Germany. Thus far, however,
it has not been an important issue in any case of recognition. Although
our State Department announced the existence of Soviet influence in
the government of Guatemala and later in that of Cuba, this occurred
after recognition had been granted. When the eventual break with
Cuba came, it was, officially at least, because of "impossible" limitations which Cuba insisted on imposing on the size of our staff in
Havana. Whether or not the United States forced a showdown will
have to remain unanswered. Finally, our delay and careful investigation
before recognizing the new regime that came to power in El Salvador
on October 25, 1960, was apparently due to concern over its possible
pro-Castro sympathies.[72]

The intrusion of the cold war into this hemisphere has presented
yet another dilemma for the United States. On the horns of this
dilemma the United States has been forced to seek refuge in the American Doctrine of Recognition. On the one hand there is a realization
that adverse opinion in Latin America, created by arbitrary acts on
the part of our government, serves to strengthen the position of ex-
tremist and nationalist groups, thereby creating a more favorable environment for the extension of Soviet influence. Our use of recognition as a political instrument runs the risk of doing just that. But the
impact of the social and economic movements already described puts
us in a "damned if you do" and "damned if you don't" position. It is
still true that if the United States withholds recognition from even a
dictatorial regime, it will be subject to bitter criticism. But if it *extends*
recognition, it will be criticized even more bitterly by a far more vocal
though perhaps smaller group.

Both the dilemma and the curious policy we have been forced to
follow are demonstrated by our action with regard to the military
dictatorship that came to power in Venezuela in 1948. In extending
recognition, a spokesman for the State Department noted that it had

delayed for two months in order to make it "abundantly clear" that it considered forcible overthrow deplorable and that, in the view of the government, "the use of force as an instrument of political change is not only deplorable but usually [note use of word "usually"] inconsistent with the acknowledged ideals of the American republics."[73] It emphasized that "this act of resuming diplomatic relations with the *de facto* Government of Venezuela is being taken as a result of an exchange of views with other American republics over a period of several weeks" and "does not imply any judgment whatsoever as to the domestic policy of such a government."[74]

Needless to say, powerful domestic interests within the United States no less than concern for the reaction of Latin American opinion urged recognition. But an unfavorable reaction could also be expected from other quarters in Latin America. Under the circumstances, the American Doctrine of Recognition was a convenient refuge.*

The inter-American system confronts the problem

We have already noted the resolution that Guatemala presented to the Inter-American Conference on Problems of War and Peace held at Mexico City in 1945.[75] At this same conference Ecuador submitted a project containing the basic principles of the Estrada Doctrine. In this project the practice of recognition was declared abolished; the establishment of *de facto* governments would in no way affect the continuity of preexisting diplomatic relations.[76]

The conference referred both projects to the Inter-American Juridical Committee for a report to the next (ninth) International Conference of American States. The subsequent report of the Committee, although a proper juridical interpretation, ignores the real factors that had prompted Guatemala to submit the resolution in the first place. Taking the words of the resolution at their face value, the Committee's

---

* The overthrow by the military of a constitutional government in Argentina in 1962 brought discrete indications of disapproval from the Kennedy administration, but recognition was extended without significant delay. Later that year a similar situation in Peru brought an explicit statement of disapproval, and the delay in extending recognition was obviously intended to make this clear. Support from most Latin Americans who had in the past loudly condemned United States recognition of dictators was now surprisingly absent. Such lack of support has demonstrated the dilemma of many Latin American liberal reformers no less than the irresponsible nature of a great deal of criticism of United States recognition policies.

report notes that it had been submitted before the triumph of the
United Nations and had been inspired by a sentiment of defense
against the dark forces of dictatorships. Since the 1945 conference, in
deciding to leave the resolution until the next International Conference
of American States, obviously did not regard it as an acceptable wartime measure, "it is not easy to see how its merits would be improved
as a measure of peace, when the danger which it would eliminate has
practically ceased to exist."[77] Furthermore, the Committee's report
noted that there now existed international instruments to deal with
threats to the peace and that such threats do not arise solely from
antidemocratic regimes.[78]

But the real purpose of the Guatemalan resolution, concerted action
against the remaining oligarchic dictatorships in the hemisphere, was
obscured by the form in which it was presented. In inter-American
affairs, the more controversial projects are usually presented in the
form of a measure to protect the peace and solidarity of the hemisphere. While they may indeed be related to this fundamental purpose,
it is not difficult to perceive some more immediate national interest
under this respectable cloak. Thus the resolution was disposed of but
the problem remained.

In addition to the Committee's report, a number of national projects
were submitted to the Ninth International Conference of American
States. A Brazilian project called upon the Executive Council of the
Pan American Union to decide whether a newly established *de facto*
government merited the establishment of diplomatic relations. Such
decisions would be merely "informative."[79] A Peruvian project called
for an exchange of opinion among American states whenever the
problem of a *de facto* regime arises.[80] Uruguay submitted a statement
of principle: "Recognition is a function of control exercised by the
international community in order to verify the conformity of the
activity of social forces with the demands of international solidarity
imposed by social fact, that is, by the existence of the international
community."[81] Mexico submitted a project which reiterated the essential principles of the Estrada Doctrine.[82]

Out of these conflicting proposals a working group produced two
compromise projects. One of them recommended an exchange of information concerning the advisability of extending recognition to a
de facto government, such exchange constituting no obligation to act
in concert.[83] The other project resolved to submit the question once
again to the Inter-American Council of Jurists with the proviso that
it consider, among other things, the possibility of collective recogni-

tion.[84] The recommendation in the first project was rejected, and the second project was approved only after striking out the only important part—the recommendation that collective recognition be considered.[85]

Another resolution, approved by the conference, contained an important statement of principle. It stated that (1) the continuity of diplomatic relations is desirable, (2) the practice of recognition should not be used as a means of individually obtaining unjustified advantages under international law, and (3) recognition of a government does not imply any judgment upon the domestic policy of that government.[86] Although subject to abuse through interpretation, point two of the resolution is a good statement of what had come to be considered an obligatory precept in this hemisphere. But, as was true of the principle of legitimacy, it received its most explicit statement only after the international order that made its application possible had been subjected to serious challenges.

Thus the problem was handed over to the newly created Inter-American Council of Jurists. A resolution approved at its first meeting noted that "divergent opinions of doctrine were expressed on essential points, excluding the possibility of reaching at this meeting a formula acceptable to an absolute majority of the representatives of the member states."[87] A resolution of its second meeting noted that "an almost unanimous opinion has been expressed to the effect that it is as yet premature to conclude a convention on the subject, and that neither is it opportune for an American inter-governmental organization to state at this time in declarative form the various principles which have been expounded by writers from time to time to govern the practice to be followed by States in this respect."[88] With these prospects in mind, the Preparatory Committee for the Tenth Inter-American Conference decided to remove the topic from the agenda for that conference, noting that there was no new aspect of the question which would justify its inclusion.[89]

In August 1960, the foreign ministers of the American states met for consultation on the problem of the Dominican Republic. Technically, the meeting was called under the Rio Pact[90] and was to deal with the problem of aggression against Venezuela committed by the Dominican Republic. The *Final Act* which called upon all the American States to sever diplomatic relations with the Trujillo regime was also technically a response to acts of aggression.[91] There is much to suggest, however, that this action had roots far deeper than this. We have already noted that, in the years following World War II, the

Trujillo regime had been a target for victorious social revolutionary movements in the Caribbean and Central America, that revolutionary governments had refused to carry on diplomatic relations with this regime and that they had urged the other American states to follow their example.

There was probably ample proof that the Dominican government had been involved in the attempts to overthrow the Venezuelan government and to assassinate President Betancourt. But it is open to question whether the record of the former is so much worse in this respect than that of some other governments in the area that such action would be justified in this instance and not in others.[92] Thus there is reason to believe that the nature of the Trujillo regime played an important part in the decision. Governments of countries where the Trujillo regime was detested by popular opinion could satisfy popular demands without establishing a precedent of severing diplomatic relations on these grounds. The Dominican Foreign Minister, sensing the climate of opinion, announced at a news conference held during the meeting that his government would hold municipal elections the following month and a presidential election within three years.[93] That the nature of the Trujillo regime as much as any specific acts of aggression was behind the move to sever diplomatic relations was further suggested by a subsequent decision of the Council of the O.A.S. calling for economic sanctions even though, as the six abstainers pointed out, there had been no further acts of aggression to justify them.[94]

At present there are no formal arrangements for handling individual cases of recognition on a collective basis. Informal consultations are usually held; and when a sensitive case is presented, the United States seems to have settled on a formula of extending recognition after a number of Latin American states have done so.

The American Doctrine in a troubled hemisphere

The American Doctrine of Recognition emerged during a revolutionary era and was an answer to the needs of the newly created American states. The British quickly saw the advantages in applying the doctrine in Latin America and, once this was done, other Great Powers soon followed Britain's lead. For nearly a hundred years the doctrine squared with both national and private interests of the American states. But after nearly a century of general application, the same private interests in the United States as well as reasons of national security required that the doctrine be replaced by one which imposed various standards of "legitimacy." After the 1930's, the doctrine again received general application in inter-American affairs.

Another revolutionary era is now bringing into question the very doctrine that emerged as a response to the needs of radical change. Rapid and revolutionary changes within national societies throughout Latin America are having a profound effect on attitudes toward the doctrine which was once generally accepted. The changes within these national societies are creating new elites and new national interests which appear to be better served by demanding new standards of "legitimacy" as the price for recognition.

Like those manifested at Vienna, contemporary attitudes toward recognition show the same realization of the intimate connection between domestic affairs and the relations between states. Thus there is renewed pressure to use recognition as an instrument for bringing about some desired condition (or preventing it) within a state. In this sense, contemporary attitudes toward recognition are a reversion to the old ideas of "legitimacy." But whereas at Vienna the object was primarily that of *preventing* change, the new doctrines of "legitimacy" are usually concerned with *promoting* change. Efforts to apply these doctrines through collective inter-American action will no doubt continue. Thus far they have been too much complicated by suspicions growing out of past experiences, the antagonisms of social revolution and the requirements of national security imposed by the cold war to offer much hope for success.

In an era no less revolutionary than the one which produced the American Doctrine of Recognition, we see many of the American states showing an ambivalent attitude. The social revolution being felt throughout Latin America has produced cleavages among classes and among nations, making it quite impossible to insulate the practice of recognition from the exigencies of politics. At the same time the struggle between the United States and the U.S.S.R. becomes inextricably linked with the social revolutionary movements.

On the one hand, the United States finds it expedient at times to justify its policy by pointing to the principles expressed in the American Doctrine, particularly when recognition of an old-style military dictatorship is involved. But the very facts that have made it expedient to do so (the irreconcilable antagonisms growing out of social revolutions) render the doctrine less useful, since the doctrine has come under question from these very movements. Where revolutionary movements directed against the old order are at least temporarily victorious, there is a strong tendency to use recognition as a political weapon. On the other hand, the United States can perceive of situations on the horizon in which it might be useful to fall back on some doctrine of "neo-legitimacy." Experience during World War II and recent events in Central America and the Caribbean have emphasized this. But too many Latin American governments are still concerned that unsheathing of this weapon for use by the O.A.S. might open too many dangerous possibilities. There are still vivid memories of its use by the United States and a fear of revival under the cloak of the O.A.S. Thus the United States runs the risk of suspicion if it supports too strongly any general plan for collective recognition.

The cold war and social revolutionary movements thus confront the American Doctrine of Recognition on a common plane. In all such revolutionary periods law is likely to be replaced by political activity, both within national societies and on the international level as well. It is little wonder, then, that so frail a thing as the American Doctrine should bend before these forces after having served a useful function during other periods.

FOOTNOTES

1. This particular term is used because it was in the Americas that the doctrine first received its most explicit pronouncement and most widespread application. It should not be taken to refer to a doctrine peculiar to *United States* policy. For a similar use of the term see William L. Neumann, *Recognition of Governments in the Americas* (Washington, 1947).

2. "It first appears as a dynastic legitimacy somewhat in the sense in which Talleyrand used it, as the theory which upheld the established hereditary right of a single house against all other single claimants. Later this theory developed into the broader principle which maintained the supremacy of monarchic government. Finally, we shall see that the concept passed beyond these special phases into a legitimacy of existing government as against all other forms of government." Julius Goebel, *The Recognition Policy of the United States* (New York, 1915), p. 10.

3. H. Lauterpacht, *Recognition in International Law* (Cambridge, 1947), p. 103.

4. J. B. Moore, *Digest*, I, p. 120.

5. William W. Kaufman, *British Policy and the Independence of Latin America, 1804–1828* (New Haven, Conn., 1951), p. 201.

6. For a discussion of economic and political considerations which brought France to extend recognition, see William Spence Robertson, *France and Latin American Independence* (Baltimore, 1939), chapters 12, 15 and 16.

7. J. Fred Rippy, *Globe and Hemisphere* (Chicago, 1958), pp. 30 ff. "The aggregate [of U.S. Capital invested] by the end of 1914 exceeded $3.5 billion,

nearly five times the total at the close of 1897, . . . well above $1.6 billion in Latin America."

8. D. Andres Bello, *Princípios de derecho internacional* (1883), pp. 48 ff.; Carlos Calvo, *Derecho internacional teórico y práctico de Europa y América* (1868), pp. 328 ff.; Charles G. Fenwick, "The Problem of Recognition of *de Facto* Governments," *Inter-American Juridical Yearbook,* 1948 (1949), pp. 19 ff.

9. J. F. Rippy, *op. cit.*, pp. 30 ff.

10. C. C. Hyde, *International Law* (2nd ed., 1947), I, p. 163.

11. W. L. Neumann, *op. cit.*, pp. 7 ff.

12. *Ibid.*

13. As with Mexico in 1913, G. H. Hackworth, *Digest,* I, p. 258; Haiti in 1911 and 1913, *ibid.,* pp. 249–252; Nicaragua in 1910, *ibid.,* p. 264; Venezuela in 1908, *ibid.,* p. 280. See also Hyde, *op. cit.,* pp. 165 ff.

14. *Foreign Relations of the U. S.,* 1913, p. 71.

15. See his letter to T. Coxe, quoted in Saul K. Padover, *Thomas Jefferson on Democracy* (New York, 1946), p. 154.

16. Lauterpacht, *op. cit.,* argues that this had been Jefferson's policy and that of subsequent administrations also. But he is forced to the absurd rationalization that "at times it was reduced to the barest minimum by being interpreted as compatible with mere passive submission to the successful government." For the more accurate position see Hyde, *op. cit.,* pp. 168 ff.; Neumann, *op. cit.,* pp. 14 ff.; Ti-Chiang Chen, *The International Law of Recognition* (New York, 1951), pp. 107 ff. For a discussion of an earlier, but indecisive, attempt to introduce a policy of "constitutional" or "republican" legitimacy under Secretary of State William H. Seward, see *ibid.,* and Stuart A. MacCorkle, *American Policy of Recognition Towards Mexico* (Baltimore, 1933), pp. 1924. The Tobar Doctrine, pronounced in 1907, has not been discussed here inasmuch as this seems to have been intended more to remove the pretext for foreign intervention than to promote a particular form of government. See discussion of Ecuadoran delegate at the Ninth Inter-American Conference.

17. "In effect it declared constitutional government to be the only government compatible with the fulfillment of international obligations on the part of Mexico, with the civilized development of Mexico herself, and with the maintenance of tolerable political economic conditions in Central America." John L. McMahon, *Recent Changes in The Recognition Policy of the United States* (Washington, D.C., 1933), *op. cit.,* p. 55.

18. Neumann, *op. cit.,* p. 19. As late as 1925, however, Secretary of State Kellogg informed the Minister from Ecuador that it had been the policy of the United States to delay the recognition of revolutionary governments as in the case of Chile in order to encourage constitutional and stable governments; Hackworth, *op. cit.,* p. 245. In 1923, the United States expressed its endorsement of the Central American Treaty of that year, by which the parties agreed not to recognize governments coming to power by extraconstitutional means. Thus in some cases the United States refused to extend recognition to Central American governments on grounds of the treaty. This treaty and a similar treaty signed in 1907 were largely a reaction to disorderly political conditions in the area and were intended more to enforce orderly changes in government than to prescribe any particular form of government. See Luis

Anderson, *El gobierno de facto* (San José, C. R., 1925), pp. 26 ff. and Chen, *op. cit.*, pp. 108 ff.

19. Luis Anderson, *op. cit.*; L. A. Podestá Costa, "Los gobiernos de facto," *Revista argentina de derecho internacional*, I (Sept.–Oct. 1920), pp. 22–23; Carlos Arangua Rives, *La intervención: doctrinas de Monroe, Drago y Tobar* (Santiago, Chile, 1925); J. M. Yepes, *La codificación del derecho internacional americano* (Bogotá, 1927) pp. 167 ff.; Isidoro Ruiz Moreno, *Lecciones de derecho internacional público* (Buenos Aires, 1935), I, pp. 111 ff.; Manuel Calero, *The Mexican Policy of President Woodrow Wilson as it Appears to a Mexican* (New York, 1916); Neumann, *op. cit.*, pp. 20 ff.
20. 20 *AJIL* (1926), Special Supplement, p. 310.
21. 22 *AJIL* (1928), Special Supplement, p. 241.
22. Samuel Flagg Bemis, *The Latin American Policy of the United States* (New York, 1943), p. 249.
23. *Ibid.*, pp. 251 ff.; Inter-American Conference, Sixth, *Diario*, pp. 486 ff. A point generally overlooked, however, is the fact that the conference did adopt the provision that "States have the right of being represented before each other through diplomatic officers," in the Convention on Diplomatic Officers; M. O. Hudson, *International Legislation*, IV, p. 2388.
24. U.S. Department of State, *Proceedings* of the United States–Mexican Commission convened in Mexico City, May 14, 1923 (Washington, D.C., 1925).
25. 25 *AJIL* (1931), Supplement, p. 203.
26. See Instituto Americano de Derecho y Legislación Comparada, *La opinión universal sobre la Doctrina Estrada* (1931).
27. Dexter Perkins, *Hands Off: A History of the Monroe Doctrine* (Boston, 1941), p. 348.
28. See vol. I, pp. 308 ff.
29. *Ibid.*, p. 308.
30. See lengthy exchange of notes between Bolivia and other governments reprinted in Bolivia, Ministerio de Relaciones Exteriores, *Boletín* (July–Dec. 1946). See also Neumann, *op. cit.*, pp. 29 ff.
31. *Foreign Relations of the U. S.*, 1936, V, p. 233.
32. *Ibid.*, p. 235.
33. *Ibid.*
34. *Ibid.*
35. *Foreign Relations of the U. S.*, 1937, V, pp. 278 ff.
36. *Ibid.*, p. 263.
37. *Ibid.*, p. 270. For similar cases see Hackworth, *op. cit.*, pp. 246–247 (Ecuador); *ibid.*, p. 270 (Paraguay). "These cases, revealing the fairly recent views of the Department of State, exemplify theories that have long prevailed," Hyde, *op. cit.*, p. 180.
38. Arthur P. Whitaker, *The United States and Argentina* (Cambridge, Mass., 1954), pp. 57 ff.; John L. Johnson, *Political Change in Latin America* (Stanford, Calif., 1958), pp. 94 ff.
39. L. M. Moreno Quintana, *La diplomacia de Irigoyen* (La Plata, Argentina, 1928), p. 82.
40. *Ibid.*, p. 84.
41. Ronald M. Schneider, *Communism in Guatemala, 1944–1954* (New York, 1958), p. 16.

42. Arévalo, quoted in Martz, *Central America: The Crisis and The Challenge* (Chapel Hill, N.C., 1959), p. 30.
43. Reprinted in International Conference of American States, Ninth, *Actas y Documentos*, V, pp. 440–441.
44. *New York Times*, June 4, 1947.
45. *Ibid.*, July 9, 1947.
46. *Ibid.*, Dec. 28, 1947.
47. *Ibid.*, Jan. 2, 1948.
48. Venezuela, Ministerio de Relaciones Exteriores, *Libro Amarillo, 1946–1947*, III, XII. The report makes no reference here to the United Nations General Assembly resolution of December 12, 1946, recommending that members recall their ambassadors and ministers from Madrid.
49. *Libro Amarillo, 1948–1952*, p. x.
50. *La Prensa* (Lima), Aug. 14, 1959.
51. *New York Times*, April 1, 1960.
52. *Hispanic World Report*, Dec. 1948, p. 18.
53. *Ibid.*
54. *Hispanic World Report*, Jan. 1948, p. 18.
55. *New York Times*, Feb. 2, 1949.
56. *Ibid.*, June 4, 1947.
57. *Ibid.*
58. Edwin Lieuwen, *Arms and Politics in Latin America* (New York, 1960), pp. 90 ff., 94 ff.; Martz, *op. cit.*, pp. 80 ff., 264 ff.
59. *Infra*, p. 20.
60. *New York Times*, June 27, 1959.
61. Guatemala, Ministerio de Relaciones Exteriores, *Carta Aérea*, Dec. 28, 1959.
62. *New York Times*, March 31, 1960.
63. *Ibid.*, Nov. 13, 1960.
64. *Ibid.*, June 16, 1961.
65. See Resolution XVII of the *Final Act*, in *Conferencias Internacionales Americanas, Primer Suplemento*, 1938–1942, p. 195.
66. The Committee was empowered "to study the problems relating to the political defense of the continent in its broadest scope, and to recommend measures intended to give effect to this object." See Carl B. Spaeth and William Sanders, "The Emergency Advisory Committee for Political Defense," 38 *AJIL* (1944), p. 221.
67. *Ibid.*, pp. 226 ff.; Neumann, *op. cit.*, pp. 32–44.
68. *Ibid.* "Four days after the revolution occurred, the Committee adopted a resolution which supplied both the policy and the procedural needs: it recommended that, for the duration of the war, the American governments agree not to accord recognition to any new government established by force, prior to full exchange of information and consultation among themselves. . . ."
69. *Ibid.*, pp. 39 ff. See also Sumner Wells, *The Time for Decision* (New York, 1944), for a strong criticism of United States policy in this connection.
70. U.S. Department of State, *Bulletin* (July 30, 1944), p. 108.
71. *New York Times*, April 20, 1946.
72. *Ibid.*, Nov. 12, Nov. 30, Dec. 4, Dec. 18, 1960.
73. *Ibid.*, Jan. 22, 1949.
74. U.S. Department of State, *Bulletin* (Feb. 6, 1949), pp. 172–173.

75. *Supra*, p. 17.
76. Inter-American Conference, Ninth, *Actas y documentos*, V, p. 441.
77. *Ibid.*, p. 441.
78. *Ibid.*, p. 445.
79. *Ibid.*, p. 463.
80. *Ibid.*, pp. 468–469.
81. *Ibid.*, p. 472.
82. *Ibid.*, p. 446.
83. *Ibid.*, II, p. 458.
84. *Ibid.*
85. Resolution XXXVI of the *Final Act, ibid.*
86. Resolution XXXV of the *Final Act.*
87. Inter-American Council of Jurists, First Meeting, *Final Act*, p. 13.
88. Inter-American Council of Jurists, Second Meeting, *Final Act*, p. 10.
89. Organization of American States, Council, *Acta de la sesión extraordinário celebrada el 10 de noviembre de 1953*, p. 1267.
90. U.S. Department of State, *Bulletin* (Sept. 5, 1960), pp. 355–359. Officially, the Inter-American Treaty of Reciprocal Assistance, signed at Rio de Janeiro September 2, 1947. After providing that "an armed attack against any American State shall be considered as an attack against all the American States," it provides that "The Organ of Consultation shall meet without delay for the purpose of . . . agreeing upon measures of a collective character that should be taken."
91. *Ibid.*
92. See, for example, Pan American Union, *Aplicaciones del Tratado Inter-Americano de Asistencia Recíproca, 1948–1958* (1959).
93. *New York Times*, Aug. 17, 1960.
94. *Ibid.*, Jan. 5, 1961.

Chapter Three

The Treatment of Aliens
and Their Property

The problem of the alien and his property

In no area of inter-American relations has there been a more serious clash of interests than in matters relating to aliens and their property. Here the conflicting currents of political and economic interests are reflected in diametrically opposed doctrines concerning a state's obligations.

Since the beginning of the multistate system, international law has of necessity left to each state jurisdiction not only over its own nationals but over aliens within its territory as well. But states have also claimed a right and even a duty to offer certain protection to their own subjects who are in the territory of another state. A more fruitful source of conflict would be difficult to find.

Among European states, whose practice became the main source of modern international law, there was a large measure of consensus on fundamental principles of justice—including respect for rights of private property. This consensus was especially strong among the ruling elites of these countries, who shared a common educational and religious background. The United States with its inherited European traditions quite naturally shared these attitudes. Thus, among these states, there was a minimum of conflict over the treatment of aliens and their property. The generally ordered conditions within each of these states of course contributed to this.

In addition to their agreement on so-called "universal standards of justice," these states shared something else. Their early economic development soon led to increased activity in non-European lands, which meant that increasing numbers of their subjects would reside in remote and often unfriendly places. The growing overseas financial investments were left at the mercy of the local governments.

Europe and the United States soon began to demand the standards of "justice" which their continued economic penetration required. They quite naturally fell back on "universal" or "internationally accepted" principles of justice, a certain minimum supposedly required by international law. But this "minimum" quite naturally reflected European (and United States) concepts and practices.

In Asia, the Middle East and parts of Africa the conflict led to a number of treaties (sometimes called "capitulations") which provided that European and United States subjects in these Asian and African states would remain wholly under the jurisdiction of their home states. Latin America also became a trouble spot, but here it was more often chronic disorder rather than disagreement on fundamental concepts of justice and property rights that was the source of trouble. Rather than capitulations, the United States and Europe relied on *ad hoc* measures of diplomatic interposition and, where this failed, armed intervention.

The main categories among the thousands of Latin American cases show the sources of trouble.[1] Diplomatic claims were brought where there was an alleged

1. Failure to offer adequate police protection, resulting in mistreatment of aliens by hostile local citizens or revolutionary activity.

2. Failure on the part of public authorities to take appropriate punitive measures against offenders by apprehending and trying them when the original offense could not reasonably have been prevented.

3. Failure to offer adequate procedural and substantive justice to aliens subjected to criminal or civil action.

4. Failure to offer adequate procedural and substantive justice to aliens bringing action on public or private contracts. This would include cases where courts refused to review executive or legislative decrees abrogating a contract or expropriating private property. If the decrees themselves, or the way in which they were applied, did not offer what the alien regarded as "prompt and adequate compensation," and if a satisfactory remedy was not available in the courts, the alien would ask his government to submit a diplomatic claim.

Controversies began almost as soon as the Latin American countries proclaimed independence, and few, if any, Latin American countries have escaped serious difficulties with the United States and Europe on this score. After the beginning of the twentieth century, in the so-called period of "dollar diplomacy" (and even after), the United States took upon itself the job of trying to enforce the traditional interpretation of state responsibility toward aliens, even where the interests involved were European.

Financial engagements contracted by unscrupulous dictators with equally unscrupulous foreign creditors accounted for a large number of claims. Successor governments which inherited these untidy financial deals quite understandably preferred to repudiate them, but in other instances a bankrupt treasury left little opportunity for choice. The history of Mexico reveals some particularly sordid transactions. Her first foreign loan (from British creditors) of 16,000,000 pesos netted her only 6,000,000 pesos. Not long after this a Swiss-French banking firm lent a nominal 75,000,000 francs to Mexico, of which the latter received only 3,750,000 francs. Incidentally, the French government used non-payment of 100 percent of this loan as part of the justification for imposition of the Maximilian regime.[2] Similar cases in other Latin American countries have given the diplomatic protection of creditors a distinctly unpleasant appearance throughout the area.[3]

Often chaotic conditions made it quite impossible for the central government to insure adequate protection to aliens no matter how seriously it tried. Under these circumstances foreign diplomatic protection and armed intervention only made the task of Latin American governments that much more difficult. At other times there was clearly a lack of proper concern on the part of both local and national authorities.

With the development of more stable economic and political conditions in Latin America, the conflicts over state responsibility have been modified. The physical protection of the alien and his property, the apprehension and trial of perpetrators of violence and the judicial procedures applied to aliens accused of misconduct are no longer a major source of trouble. Even the old problem of default and repudiation of public debts (owed to private creditors) is no longer a major one. The process of freeing the Department of State from the job of helping United States holders of Latin American government bonds to collect full payment was largely completed under the Hoover administration.

The more serious disputes now arise from such direct state actions as the outright expropriation of private property or the legislative or administrative revision of concessionary rights through changes in taxes and other fees and through labor and social legislation which affects these rights. Not only are these disputes by their very nature far more explosive than their predecessors, but also there is every indication that they will increase rather than decrease during the next decade. It is no longer simply a case of a military or oligarchic dictator repudiating the debt contracted by an unscrupulous predecessor, a matter which in the past occasioned relatively little public attention. Expropriation of property for land reform or to place a monopoly "in the hands of the nation," by contrast, becomes a matter intimately linked with revolutionary programs of social reform. It may become a symbol of national aspirations for liberation from foreign economic domination at the same time that it becomes a symbol of the liberation of the masses from domination by a local oligarchy. Under these circumstances the new revolutionary leader will not be as easily persuaded to back down in the face of diplomatic intervention as was the traditional Latin American dictator.

Equally significant is the fact that the ruling elites who in the past held the reins of power in Latin America were the owners of landed wealth (as were their military allies who had a way of quickly becoming landowners). As such they quite naturally looked with favor on the institution of private property and the legal norms that protected it. Not so with the new revolutionary elites who, on the contrary, find it necessary to change the structure of ownership. They must do so not only to offer some evidence of the sincerity of their promises to the masses but also to break the power of the opposition.

The United States has consistently taken the position that expropriation is legitimate but that prompt, effective and adequate compensation must follow. Latin Americans have generally insisted that they would offer prompt and adequate compensation (though not always agreeing that they were obliged to) but have insisted that they alone had the right to determine what constituted "prompt and adequate."[4] Attempts to revise contracts, usually with regard to taxes, royalties or labor relations, have sometimes ended in outright expropriation. The refusal of an industry to accept what it regards as outrageous demands may lead to strikes or shutdowns. If the industry is a major part of the national economy, the government may insist on taking over. Then the same problem of compensation arises.

Four of the more notable cases involving the expropriation of private property in Latin America will show the difficulty of trying to fit this revolutionary situation into the mold of traditional legal norms.

Social revolution versus traditional rules

The Mexican Revolution of 1910 introduced into this hemisphere the contemporary phase of the problem of state responsibility toward aliens and their property. Though no two revolutionary movements are precisely the same, the forces behind this revolution and their impact upon the question of state responsibility have been present in subsequent Latin American social revolutions. There is good reason to believe that the pattern will be repeated.

Under the iron-fisted dictatorship of Porfirio Díaz, Mexico had become a splendid place for foreigners and for a very few Mexicans who occupied the small but plush "room at the top." The peasants, a majority of the population, lived in the most abject state of servitude. Even Indian communal lands which had survived Spanish exploitation found their way into hands of the large landowners, with the aid of Díaz' new laws.[5]

A small middle sector, which had once occupied an important position in the commercial life of the country, saw foreigners rapidly taking over major sectors of the nation's economy. By 1910, nearly one-half of Mexico's total national wealth was owned by foreigners. Foreign ownership of mineral resources was even more concentrated than that of agricultural lands. Mexico's natural resources had been dispensed with a bountiful and easy hand. To be sure, it had all been done "legally" as far as the foreign investors were concerned. But it was "law" created by Díaz, enforced by his army and police and used in the interest of a tiny minority.[6]

When Mexican revolutionaries looked back on the spectacle of oil men dealing with ignorant peasants who had little comprehension of the potential value of their land, when they looked back on the use of force and bribery (with the benevolent cooperation of Díaz), would they be likely to hold this kind of "law" in very high esteem? Spanish law had reserved important subsoil minerals to the Crown and successive Mexican governments had reiterated their rights to these deposits. Díaz changed all of this in order to attract foreign investment and, needless to say, his wisdom was proclaimed in financial circles throughout the world.[7] But how would the more educated Mexican revolutionaries look upon "laws" that marked so sharp a break with Mexican legal tradition? Finally, would they make a distinction between these deals and the many unquestionably scrupulous ones?

The answer came as the revolution slowly devastated the country. In the lower levels it came with the cry for "land and bread." In the higher levels it came with the slogan "Mexico for the Mexicans." The shouting was eventually crystalized in the lengthy Constitution of 1917, a document which laid the groundwork for a United States–Mexican controversy that dragged on for more than two decades. For our purposes, the most important part of this constitution was the now famous Article 27, which contained these two fundamental principles.

(1) The ownership of all lands and waters were vested originally in the nation, which could transmit title to private persons and thereby create private property. All such property could be regulated in the public interest and expropriated for reasons of public utility upon payment of indemnification.

(2) Direct ownership of all minerals and various other subsoil properties, including petroleum and all hydrocarbons, was vested in the nation. Compensation or "indemnification" was not mentioned here.

Article 27 specifically referred to the necessity of dividing up large landholdings for a more equitable distribution of the public wealth—and well it might, in a country where virtually all the arable land was owned by 3 or 4 percent of the population. The mild efforts to implement these provisions shortly after 1917 brought protests from the United States over land taken from its citizens without compensation. The program of land distribution was greatly speeded up under the regime of Lazaro Cárdenas (1934–1940) and, since payment was not provided, so were the protests from the United States Department of State.[8]

In 1938, an additional source of conflict was added which, for the time being, overshadowed even the problems arising out of the agricultural expropriations. Labor, with the blessing of Cárdenas, began to make new demands on the petroleum industry, not only for increased pay and social benefits but for inclusion of Mexicans in the white-collar office forces as well. The petroleum industry pronounced these demands "impossible" and refused to capitulate. On May 28, 1937, the oil workers went out on strike, the industry shut down and the serious effects on the Mexican economy were quickly felt. In accordance with Mexican labor law, the matter was submitted to the federal Board of Conciliation and Arbitration, whereupon the strike was ended provisionally. The Board's report, although not granting all of labor's demands, found most of them legitimate. In February 1938, President Cárdenas left the matter up to the Supreme Court, which quickly handed down a decision unanimously upholding the decision of the labor board. The companies then issued a statement that "their inability to comply remains unaltered by today's verdict." Shortly thereafter Cárdenas expropriated the industry, declaring that "in view of the rupture of the contracts between the companies and their workers . . . an immediate paralysis of the oil industry is imminent, implying incalculable damage to all other industry and the general economy of the country." [9]

In the legal gymnastics that followed, Mexico agreed that she was obligated to provide compensation *but only as provided under her own laws and constitution.* "My Government maintains," said the Mexican Foreign Minister, "that there is in international law no rule universally accepted in theory nor carried out in practice, which makes obligatory the payment of immediate compensation nor even of deferred compensation, for expropriations of a general and impersonal character like those which Mexico has carried out for the redistribution of land."[10] And as far as the oil companies were concerned: "Mexico is willing to settle 'in justice and equity' *under Mexican law.* . . . We shall pay every dollar or pound that has been put into the properties we have taken over. We do not, however, regard the oil expropriation as a matter for diplomatic intervention or discussion."[11]

Thus Mexico argued that, since her only obligation to compensate arose under her own constitution and laws, she alone must determine the extent and time of such compensation and no international question was involved. The United States argued that there was a generally accepted rule of international law requiring prompt, effective and adequate compensation and that an international question therefore existed. Here the legal arguments rested while the dispute simmered on.

Three factors conditioned and hardened the Mexican attitude toward these expropriations. First, many (but certainly not all) of the hotly disputed oil and agricultural concessions had been granted under the notorious land-grabs of the regime of Porfirio Díaz. Although, strictly speaking, most of them were probably legal, they were legal under laws promulgated by Díaz in order to enrich a few supporters. Hence the laws often clearly ran contrary to what might be called the community's sense of justice. Indian communities were deprived of their communal lands by convenient legal technicalities, and Díaz' new petroleum laws reversed centuries of Spanish and Mexican tradition which left important subsoil properties to the state.

Second, investors put forth ridiculously high claims which were generally accepted at face value by the State Department. Sumner Welles frankly admitted to a Mexican official that some Americans "had acquired land for practically nothing and . . . were claiming fantastic sums for compensation." Even more absurd were the claims made by the oil companies. After the State Department had for nearly three years supported their demands for roughly $450,000,000, our own Department of Interior experts concluded in a report (which the State Department chose to keep secret) that their properties were worth no more than $25,000,000. Other independent estimates were close to this figure.[12] When arrangements were finally made for an appraisal by an impartial commission (something in which the companies were not the least bit interested), the appraiser lamented that "we insisted that Standard Oil had invested over $400,000,000 in their properties, only to have the Mexicans bring out the books of the oil companies which plainly showed they had put in much less."[13]

Third, the oil companies were concerned neither with negotiating on conditions that might have prevented expropriation nor with fair compensation once the Mexican government had expropriated. They were more interested in making it clear from the outset that they would not be subject to anything they might regard as unreasonable demands by the Mexican government.[14] "Having made big money on absurdly low wages from the time the oil gushers made Doheny and Pearson rich, all oil producers opposed any change in taxes and wages, and resent it if their government does not take their point of view. . . . As a rule, the oil men will be satisfied with nothing less than that the United States Government attempt to direct the Mexican policy for their financial benefit."[15] Thus commented the United States Ambassador to Mexico, Josephus Daniels. When Mexican Finance Minister Suárez offered to prove to them, from their tax records, that they could well afford the increased labor benefits the syndicates had demanded, the companies declined to avail themselves of the opportunity.[16]

Their original assertion that pay increases were financially impossible was made somewhat questionable by their later offer to accept nearly all of them when threatened by expropriation. But the offer was accompanied by a demand that the government sign a statement that this would be the final and maximum demand. Cárdenas regarded this as a slur on his personal honor and went ahead with the expropriation. The final offer of the stunned companies to pay the full 26,000,-000 pesos in labor benefits which had been demanded (even without the guarantees) further weakened their claim that the demands were "impossible." [17]

Recent and detailed evidence indicates that once the properties had been expropriated the companies made not the slightest move toward reaching any settlement which might establish the right of expropriation *even with fair compensation*. Rather they concentrated their efforts on creating conditions that might lead to the overthrow of the Cárdenas administration or make it back down in the face of adverse economic conditions and threatened revolt.[18] On the eve of the presentation of the report by the appraisers appointed by the United States and Mexico, a board member of Standard Oil, who had reason to fear that a reasonable appraisal would be made, came to the State Department with a last plea. Standard Oil, he said, "would be willing to see that Mexico received 50 percent of the profits through royalties, taxes, et cetera, *and that a working arrangement would be better than a fair or unfair evaluation.*"[19] This offer, it has been correctly observed, was "undoubtedly far more than would have originally been required to avert the expropriation. The only trouble was that it came about four years too late."[20]

With the crisis becoming more threatening in Europe, the United States became increasingly concerned over rumors of arrangements to sell Mexican oil to the Axis powers and of the danger of generally closer ties between these countries. The Roosevelt administration thus made it quite clear to the United States claimants that they would have to accept a compromise arrangement or stand to lose everything. In the case of the petroleum properties Roosevelt had suggested publicly that the companies should expect to receive only the actual cash sums they had invested, less depreciation, thus ruling out the extravagant claims for the value of the oil yet underground. A joint commission valued the properties at $23,995,991, to which must be added $8,500,000 that had been paid to Sinclair in a separate settlement. Compared with the $450,000,000 that the oil companies had demanded about two years earlier, this was a considerable reduction to say the least.[21]

Perhaps the most unfortunate aspect of the whole controversy was that throughout the discussions the more legitimate claims were treated on the same basis as the most notorious fabrications. Ambassador Daniels indeed tried to get the State Department to draw some distinctions but seems to have had no success.[22] Certainly a careful sifting of the claims from the very beginning would have strengthened the Department's position on those that were truly legitimate.

The Guatemalan land expropriations of 1953 were complicated by most of the circumstances that had surrounded the earlier Mexican action. All the social and economic injustices of the Mexican scene were present in Guatemala. The United Fruit Company (UFCO) in Guatemala represented the same challenge to the country's independence that the oil companies had presented in Mexico. Its importance in the Guatemalan economy made it relatively even more powerful than the Mexican oil companies had ever been.

The company had built up an impressive backlog of resentment among the masses, the intellectuals and much of the middle class, partly as a result of its very size, partly as a result of its conduct. The former needs no explanation; the latter does. There was general agreement in Guatemala, even among those most opposed to the Arbenz regime (elected in 1951), that UFCO contracts negotiated with General Ubico, the most detestable of dictators in Guatemalan history, had been negotiated at the expense of the country and were in need of drastic revision.[23] The fact that a Guatemalan dictator was as much responsible as the company made little difference to reform-minded Guatemalans; they had had enough of both partners and intended to make some changes which they felt were centuries overdue.

Not only had the company been granted ninety-nine-year concessions virtually free from taxes and other duties (a study by three United States economists estimated in 1951 that these contracts still probably left UFCO's tax liability at about one-half of what it would be in their absence).[24] To make certain that taxes would be only nominal, the company was also allowed to undervalue its properties for tax purposes and to practice price discrimination on its railroad in order to conceal its profits. Fictitious, low export prices were declared on their products sold to overseas subsidiaries, further concealing a large part of the company's profits.[25] In short,

Guatemalans, with complete justification could state that UFCO gave inadequate compensation to the government for concessions granted to it. Duties and taxes totalled one-tenth of UFCO annual profit. When Arévalo requested a new arrangement he was coldly rebuffed.[26]

Nor had the company any intentions of willingly relinquishing any of its advantages of cheap labor. When, in 1948, striking laborers asked for increased medical care, new housing and a daily wage of $1.50, UFCO's answer was a lockout. In the long series of disputes which followed, the company felt that it could not seriously be threatened by talk of expropriation in a country where it had always been more powerful than the government. "In the last analysis, the enraged attitude of the company officials usually boiled down to a dogmatic belief that 'they can't do it to us!' When 'they' did, company officials were dumbfounded."[27]

Under the 1953 Agrarian Reform Law, 234,000 acres of UFCO land were expropriated in the first move and the seizure of another 173,000 acres was ordered shortly thereafter. The Guatemalan government, according to the Agrarian Reform Law, offered compensation in twenty-five-year agrarian bonds based on the tax evaluations recorded as of May 9, 1952.[28]

The Department of State delivered a formal protest, insisting that twenty-five-year bonds at 3 percent was not "prompt" payment and that compensation based on the low tax evaluations of the past was not "adequate."[29] The Department apparently accepted the company's argument that they had for some years been trying to get the government to reevaluate these properties. What the Department apparently failed to realize was that the company made this gesture only after there were rather clear indications that expropriation was in the air.[30] Guatemala thus offered to pay some $600,000 while the company demanded $15,854,849.[31] Whether the State Department was more critical in accepting UFCO's assessment than it had been in accepting the oil companies' evaluations in Mexico remains to be seen.

The United States protests were rejected by Guatemala on the grounds that expropriation was an inherent act of sovereignty not subject to international discussion as long as there was no discrimination against aliens.[32] Here the dispute rested until the Arbenz government was overthrown in June 1954.

With a new government in power, negotiations were soon resumed between the company and the Guatemalan government. UFCO now seemed "happy" to grant much more than had originally been termed "impossible" or "unreasonable." It agreed to pay 30 percent tax on its profits (having flatly rejected 10 percent earlier) to embark upon a $5,000,000 rehabilitation program, build a one-hundred-bed hospital and grant the government 110,000 acres of its land. In addition to this, in order to encourage prompt ratification of the agreement, it agreed to pay $700,000 taxes for the year if the agreement (signed in December) was ratified before the end of the year.[33] UFCO had apparently realized that, in order to preserve most of a good thing, it would be necessary to give up some of it.

The expropriation of the Bolivian tin mines has been described as an absolute political necessity.

> The nationalization of Patiño, Aramayo, and Hochschild was an absolute political necessity. The companies were waist-deep in politics, and had been hostile to the M.N.R.* To carry out the *Movimiento Nacionalista Revolucionario's* program of economic nationalism its leaders were anxious to get into the hands of Bolivians the source of wealth which produced 80 per cent of the country's foreign exchange. Finally, the nationalization of the tin mines was a test of good faith of the M.N.R. government. If it had failed to take this step, its worker and middle-class supporters would have doubted its willingness or ability to carry out the other parts of its program.[34]

If the program of the revolution (the program of the National Revolutionary Movement which came to power in 1952) was going to be carried out, it would be necessary to get the three big companies out of politics—or so it seemed to the M.N.R. In the past, the companies had financed revolutions, subsidized candidates for office, bribed officials and made substantial contributions to the anti-M.N.R. forces in 1952.[35] There was no reason to believe that they would not resort to these tactics again, if necessary. With the mines producing 80 percent of the total Bolivian foreign exchange, the economic power of the companies was obvious.[36]

On October 31, 1952, the nationalization decree was issued. It included an indictment against the companies, referring to the dangerous concentration of economic power which had produced a concentration of political power, to privileged exemptions from taxes and to "inhuman and oppressive" labor policies.[37] The government insisted from the outset that it intended to pay for the expropriated properties;[38] the question was "How much?" Pending a final settlement, Bolivia agreed to pay the companies on account by means of discounts on the exports of tin, a percentage to vary in accordance with the price of metal.[39]

This particular question of expropriation never became a major issue in inter-American politics, one reason being that United States interests represented only a part of one of the expropriated companies

---

* *Movimiento Nacional Revolucionario*—National Revolutionary Movement.

—the Patiño mines. No formal protests were made, although "informal conversations" apparently took place.[40] Nevertheless, the United States was obviously concerned over the principle involved, and it was not until after the agreement for partial compensation (just referred to) was reached that the United States again began contracting for Bolivian tin.[41] In view of the importance of the United States as a market for this all-important Bolivian product, such a policy was clearly a not-too-subtle pressure on Bolivia to meet the demands of the tin barons.

On December 15, 1960, an agreement was reached for a final settlement with the Patiño interests. Bolivia agreed to pay $6,000,000 for the expropriated properties and Patiño in turn agreed to lend the government-owned mining corporation $5,000,000. Under the contingent arrangement referred to earlier, it was reported that the three large companies had already collected about $20,000,000. Patiño's acceptance of the financial settlement depended on passage by the Bolivian legislature of a divorce law favorable to him, a formality which was accomplished five days later.[42] The significance which international lawyers will place on this romantic aspect of the case, so far as the "law of expropriation" is concerned, is still unknown.

Settlement seems also to have been "facilitated" by the Soviet offer to assist the Bolivian government in building its own tin refinery. Bolivia's dependence on the Patiño-owned tin refinery in England had strengthened Patiño's position and had encouraged him to hold off for the most favorable settlement.[43]

Lack of detailed information makes it impossible to draw firm conclusions from the Cuban agricultural and industrial expropriations. These expropriations began with the Agrarian Reform Law of 1959, which provided for expropriation of properties over a certain size, depending on the use and yield of the property. The same law offered compensation in twenty-year agrarian bonds at $4\frac{1}{2}$ percent based on tax evaluations as of 1958.[44] Needless to say, the large landowners in Cuba had long enjoyed the practice of ludicrous tax assessments which represented only a fraction of the real value of the properties. Even the questionable argument that the owners were not at fault, since previous governments had permitted this, is a little difficult to admit here. When the Castro government asked the American owners to reassess the value of their property, they came up with the same low figures.[45]

A United States note, delivered on October 12, 1959, protested that the compensation offered was neither prompt nor adequate but gave no further details about why it took this position.[46] Later protests pointed out that expropriations were carried out without the procedural safeguards provided under the Agrarian Reform Law and the Cuban Constitution of 1940.[47] To the Cuban argument that these expropriations were an absolute political and social necessity and that existing conditions made it impossible for the government to compensate according to principles put forth in the 1940 Constitution, the United States gave essentially the same reply that it had given to Mexico nearly three decades earlier.

The factors mentioned by Your Excellency explaining the inability of the Government of Cuba to apply these principles have been noted by the Government of the United States. It is the opinion of the Government of the United States, however, that the United States investors, who are not responsible for these factors, should not, in justice, be penalized because of them; nor can such factors constitute a valid basis for the expropriation of the property of aliens in disregard of accepted principles of international law relating to payment of prompt, adequate and effective compensation.[48]

Following the passage of United States legislation which granted the President power to reduce the Cuban sugar quota, the government of Cuba issued a new nationalization law. It gave the President and Prime Minister "full powers to proceed with the nationalization of all concerns and properties of natural or juridical persons of the United States of America or of the concerns in which said persons have a majority interest or share." According to the preamble, the law was intended as retaliation for "constant aggression against the fundamental interests of the Cuban economy." It offered as evidence the sugar act just mentioned.[49] Payment was to be made out of an amortization fund collected from 25 percent of the foreign exchange corresponding to the excess of the purchase of sugar made in each calendar year by the United States over 3,000,000 long Spanish tons, for internal consumption, at a price not under 5.75 cents per pound.[50]

The next major expropriations were based on a different premise. The American-owned Texaco and Esso Standard Oil Company refineries were expropriated when they refused to refine crude oil not obtained from their own sources of supply. The United States note of protest did not discuss the matter of compensation, merely stating that the refineries represented millions of dollars of new capital and reinvestment of earnings.[51] Not long after this the United States terminated its purchases of Cuban sugar and, in retaliation for what it termed "economic aggression," the Cuban government confiscated most of the remaining United States–owned property on the island. At this point the estimated value of all United States–owned properties which had been confiscated was placed at $1,500,000,000, with another $100,000,000 worth of property still remaining in the hands of its owners.[52]

Latin reactions: the struggle for revision of the rules

Attempting to limit their international obligations toward aliens, the Latin American states have faced a formidable group of adversaries. We have already seen in the previous chapter how the weapon of nonrecognition was used by the United States and other Great Powers in order to secure some measure of compliance with their interpretation of the rules. We have also shown how Latin American efforts to eliminate the institution of recognition from the realm of inter-American politics gained a large measure of success, *de facto* if not *de jure*, only to have the problem reopened in the wake of twentieth-century social revolutions.

Two other instruments have been used by the Great Powers in securing compliance with their interpretation of the rules relating to the treatment of aliens. The first of these, armed intervention, has been all but eliminated, thanks in large part to a lengthy and concerted Latin American effort.* The second, diplomatic intervention, is still very much challenged and still very much used. Latin American efforts to eliminate or circumscribe the use of both these instruments has been a singular feature of inter-American diplomacy in the twentieth century.

As early as the nineteenth century, Latin American constitutions began to include the provision that aliens should be guaranteed equal treatment with citizens but could demand and expect no more. Clauses in contracts with foreign investors† obligated the latter to renounce their right to call upon their governments for diplomatic support. But the United States and other Great Powers refused to be bound by such

---

* Article 2 of the United Nations Charter also provides that "all members shall refrain . . . from the threat or use of force against the territorial integrity or political independence of any state." The O.A.S. Charter contains a similar provision.

† Generally referred to as "Calvo" clauses after the Argentine jurist, Carlos Calvo, who suggested such clauses to induce aliens to rely on local remedies instead of on diplomatic interposition.

measures, arguing that constitutional provisions could not unilaterally change international law and that the individual could not by contract affect his government's right to intervene.[53]

Since the desired aims have not been achieved through such measures, a major effort has been directed toward marshaling the support of Latin Americans for a statement or restatement of a set of rules more in keeping with their interests. The first concerted effort along these lines was directed at what Latin Americans considered the worst abuse—armed intervention. In a note of December 29, 1902, Dr. Luis Drago, Argentine Minister of Foreign Affairs, advanced the idea that public debts of American states ought not to be the occasion of armed intervention by European powers.[54] This principle, which came to be known as the Drago Doctrine, received nearly unanimous support in Latin America and finally received partial recognition at the Second Hague Conference in 1907. The parties to the convention signed by that conference agreed not to have recourse to armed force for the recovery of contract debts claimed as being due to their nationals. On the initiative of the United States, however, it was agreed that this undertaking is not applicable when the debtor state refuses or neglects to reply to an offer of arbitration.[55]

As far as Latin America was concerned, the Hague convention had two fatal defects. First, arbitration meant that the rules of state responsibility, with which they disagreed, would still be applied. Second, outlawing only *armed* intervention meant that other forms might still be applied. The long and bitter struggle reached a climax at the Sixth International Conference of American States held at Havana in 1928. The conference had before it a recommendation of the Commission of Jurists which stated that "no state has a right to interfere in the internal affairs of another."[56]

Actual intervention by the United States in the Caribbean together with pointed references by a number of Latin American delegations made it quite clear to whom the clause was directed. An attempt was made in committee to substitute a more innocuous statement in place of the non-intervention article, but this was vigorously opposed by the majority of Latin American delegations. Intervention by one state in the affairs of another was condemned in absolute terms by virtually all of them.[57]

When the article reached the full conference, debate was more temperate, but there is little doubt that the Argentine statement before Commission II represented the feelings of virtually all the Latin American delegations.

Sovereignty of states is the absolute right of full interior autonomy and complete external independence. That right is guaranteed to the strong nations by their power and to the weak through the respect of the strong. If that right is not consecrated and is not protected in absolute form, international juridical harmony does not exist. Intervention, diplomatic or armed, permanent or temporary, threatens the independence of states.[58]

Quite a different point of view was presented by Mr. Hughes, who clearly represented the views of a power with expanding commercial interests.

What are we going to do when government breaks down and American citizens are in danger of their lives? Are we to stand by and see them killed because a government in circumstances which it cannot control and for which it may not be responsible can no longer afford reasonable protections? . . .
Now it is a principle of international law that in such case a government is fully justified in taking action—I would call it interposition of a temporary character—for the purpose of protecting the lives and property of its nationals. I would say that it does not constitute an intervention. . . .[59]

Only one delegate, Dr. Maúrtua of Peru, urged his colleagues to think in terms less rigid than intervention or non-intervention. For this he has been the recipient of criticism by less able jurists who are still fighting the intervention battle in the light of the issues of 1928. He warned his colleagues that the guarantees which they sought were not to be found in the doctrine of absolute state sovereignty. They existed only in the juridical organization of the continent. He insisted that states could not conduct even their internal affairs "as if they lived in the desert." Sovereignty implied "the duty of sincerely practicing democracy and the republican form of government in order to assure a stable order and a regime of guarantees to all the inhabitants of its territory."[60]

But the conference was in no mood to consider measures such as this. Since a number of Latin American delegates wanted to avoid an open break, the only solution was to postpone consideration until the next meeting. Shortly after the 1928 conference, Dr. Maúrtua published an article in which he lamented the fact that his Latin American colleagues had only "pronounced against intervention in the abstract."[61] They should have considered this problem from the point of view of the interests of the American continent. International financial contracts authorizing intervention might have been placed under international supervision so that the interests of both the superior and inferior economies would be submitted to a juridical order capable of deciding such questions equitably. Fair internal legislation as well as fair investment of speculative capital should be a matter of international concern. "Independence is a right. . . . But it is not enough to proclaim and to exercise it. It is necessary to exercise it in the character of a competence which is limited by justice and the need of the community."[62]

The Seventh International Conference of American States (1933) approved the Convention on Rights and Duties of States, which contained a clause stating that "no state has the right to intervene in the internal or external affairs of another."[63] Succeeding inter-American conferences and meetings reemphasized and restated the principle in ever stronger terms.

Although resolutions and other measures stated in more and more comprehensive form that intervention of any kind was contrary to American international law, the problem was far from solved in the eyes of the Latin Americans. Diplomatic protests from a power as great as the United States were still a force to be reckoned with— especially when they made unsettled claims the grounds for delaying or suspending important commercial or financial negotiations. A frontal attack on the institution of diplomatic intervention had to be made.

At the Inter-American Conference for the Maintenance of Peace, held at Buenos Aires in 1936, an Argentine-Chilean-Peruvian proposal was endorsed by a majority of the Latin American states. It provided that "The High Contracting Parties bind themselves, without any reservation, not to use armed force *nor to have recourse to diplomatic protection,* nor accept it for collection of public or contractual debts, or for the support of claims the origin of which is exclusively pecuniary."[64] Strong United States opposition was sufficient to relegate the proposal to a committee of experts which by the usual standards of diplomatic nicety should have been the end of it.[65]

The project that this committee sent on to the Eighth International Conference of American States (Lima, 1938) was essentially the same as the 1936 proposal. But an additional clause which would have defeated what the Latin Americans had hoped to gain by it had been attached. Diplomatic intervention was permitted only if there had been a denial of justice (which had no satisfactory definition among American states), and either creditor or debtor could demand and obtain arbitration in the event of such a denial.[66] In order to bring this closer to what the Latin Americans had wanted in the first place, a majority of these states supported a memorandum which provided that there was no denial of justice if equality of treatment was offered to both alien and citizen.[67] Since the United States would not accept this solution, it was obvious that the whole proposal needed more attention from experts.

The matter did not receive serious official attention until the next inter-American conference, held at Bogotá in 1948. By this time opposition by the United States had lost some of its weight, and the Latin American states achieved a measure of success by having the following article included in the Pact of Bogotá (the American Treaty of Pacific Settlement).

The High Contracting Parties bind themselves not to make diplomatic representations in order to protect their nationals, or to refer a controversy to a court of international jurisdiction for that purpose, when said nationals have had available the means to place their case before competent domestic courts of the respective state.[68]

The reader will recognize that this is essentially the same as the 1936 proposal made at Buenos Aires, but instead of remaining silent on the matter of judicial settlement by an international tribunal, this article actually seems to bind the parties not to seek such settlement. In signing the treaty the United States affixed a reservation which flatly stated that it did not accept this article.[69]

The next (1954) conference was too occupied with problems of Communism in this hemisphere to deal directly with the question of state responsibility. In view of the fact that the International Law Commission of the United Nations was to deal with this question, the conference did, however, recommend that the Inter-American Council of Jurists prepare a study of the contribution this hemisphere has made to this question. The Inter-American Juridical Committee (the permanent committee of the Inter-American Council of Jurists) accordingly prepared a report on the *Contribution of the American Continent to the Principles of International Law That Govern the Responsibility of the State*.

Signed by all eight Latin American members of the committee and vigorously opposed by the United States delegate,[70] the report contains what Latin Americans have long sought to have established as principles of law in this hemisphere. Intervention in the internal or external affairs of a state as a sanction of the responsibility of that state was declared inadmissible. The "equality of treatment" doctrine was stated in this form: "The state is not responsible for acts or omissions with respect to aliens except in those cases where it has, under its own laws, the same responsibility toward its nationals." Finally,

a. There is no denial of justice when aliens have available the means to place their case before the competent domestic courts of the respective state.

b. The state has fulfilled its international responsibility when the judicial authority passes down its decision, even though it declares the claim, action or recourse brought by the alien to be inadmissible.

c. The state has no responsibility with regard to the judicial decision, whatever it may be, even if it is not satisfactory to the claimant.[71]

A number of Latin American states have from time to time pressed for institutional arrangements to deal with cases arising out of the conflicting doctrines of state responsibility. We have already noted Dr. Maúrtua's (Peru) proposals made at the Sixth International Conference of American States and his later references to the problem. In 1936, Mexico submitted a *Code for an Inter-American Court of Justice* to the Buenos Aires Peace Conference. "American legal controversies," the code stated, "should be decided by American judges . . . [and] a correct understanding of facts pertaining to the Americas is more readily to be obtained by Americans themselves. . . . An organization of American jurists would save us from the errors attendant upon the defective system of the Claims Commissions, providing stronger guarantees of objectivity in awards. . . ."[72]

At the Bogotá conference in 1948, there was again strong pressure for an inter-American court, but only a resolution calling for the elaboration of a statute was passed. Since that time the matter has been shuttled back and forth among conferences, committees and governments without any significant progress. The Council of the Organization of American States finally resorted to circulating a questionnaire among member governments in order to determine whether a majority felt that it was empowered to draft such a statute. Only eight governments have even bothered to reply. Of the three who replied in the negative, Chile offered no reason for her position, but Argentina and the United States felt that such a court would be a duplication of the efforts of the International Court of Justice. Cuba (in 1956), Ecuador and El Salvador replied in favor of the idea, but Brazil and Mexico did so conditionally (emphasizing that they were in no way opposed to the idea).[73]

Traditional rules, social revolution and community interest

The fundamental disagreement between the United States and its Latin American neighbors over the rules of international law applying to aliens and their property must be seen in the light of a basic conflict of interests and against a background of a century or more of irritation and resentment. A more viable set of rules can evolve only if the force of these moral, political and social data is taken into account. Thus the meticulous labors of the jurist, showing that well-established, customary rules of law require a particular treatment of aliens and their property, only help to freeze the law into positions ill-adapted to meet changing conditions. It is quite useless to talk about an impartial judicial settlement when the law itself is regarded by one of the parties as outdated, unjust and in need of revision.

The position taken by the United States and Western European countries probably presents the stronger legal case if viewed from the standpoint of customary international law.[74] This explains why Latin American states, although insisting that the law is on their side, have generally accepted a settlement by an international tribunal only when under strong pressure from a more powerful claimant. They have reason to fear that such a body will apply the rules which rely heavily on the practice of the nineteenth and early twentieth centuries. This possibility, however, is becoming less and less certain as more and more states in the world make known their opposition to the traditional rules. It has also been shown, elsewhere, that even the practice on which Europe and the United States base their position is by no means as consistent as their lawyers would make it appear.[75] But since it is obviously easier for these states to risk an adverse judgment than it would be for some shaky revolutionary government, the former appear to remain in the stronger legal position.

The real problem is that most of Latin America feels that the traditional rules a tribunal would be likely to apply are clearly unjust. Some of the factors that produced the cases discussed in the second section of this chapter help to explain *why* Latin Americans feel that application of these rules would inflict an injustice upon them. Usually these factors were not articulated in the diplomatic exchanges between the parties to the conflict simply because the traditional rules had not provided that consideration be given to them. To argue that the rules should be changed carries little weight in diplomacy and only helps to prove that the protester is the lawbreaker.

Nearly thirty years ago, Professor Frederick Dunn suggested some basic principles for a more viable set of rules. They would, he pointed out, have to rest on the assumption that "the members of the international community have, in some degree, a common interest in the carrying on of international trade and intercourse in the customary manner."[76] Normal trade and intercourse always assume a certain amount of risk and are capable of absorbing this within limits. A more viable set of rules, then, "would seek to distribute the risks where they can best be borne, with a view to creating and maintaining the minimum conditions necessary for continuance of mutually profitable inter community relationships."[77]

A new and important field of study must be undertaken by the legal and political scientist. The first step must be a more precise statement of the ends of the legal institution concerned with the protection of the alien and his property. A body of empirical knowledge about the subject must serve as the foundation for the articulation of these ends. It simply will not suffice to center exclusively on the factor of legal doctrine. We have stated the underlying purpose only in the most general terms: "to aid in the maintenance of the conditions of order and security that are essential for the carrying on of normal social and economic relations across national boundaries."[78] The assessment of these essential conditions must be made on the basis of empirical knowledge about the inter-American "community" and its individual members, not on the basis of abstract reasoning.

A second step is the restatement and rearrangement of rules and principles drawn from past practice in order to serve these ends. Certainly this step will not be an easy task. It will require a very careful and objective study of the relationship of traditional rules and practices to the social needs they have fulfilled or ignored. The social needs of national societies and of international society must be studied and balanced. The task is of course greatly complicated by the personal and national biases that plague all attempts to analyze international problems. But these biases have not prevented social scientists from working out techniques to reduce them. A number of important efforts are now being made in Western capital-exporting countries to codify and improve the law of foreign investment. The most notable effort in the United States has been the draft recently prepared for the Harvard Law School by Louis B. Sohn and R. R. Baxter.[79]

There is, first of all, the question of the meaning of "prompt and adequate" compensation. Neither theory nor practice has ever come close to anything like an objective standard.[80] The awards of arbitration and diplomatic negotiation are only as consistent as the expediency which they clothe in legal phrases. Textbook attempts to provide a standard offer fewer surprises but little more enlightenment. The tendency of the United States has too often been to accept uncritically the most notorious fabrications of investors until expediency required that a settlement be made on virtually any terms. Then the settlement has often been less advantageous to the investor than one that might have been negotiated earlier. Ground rules which give a reasonable indication of what problems may be taken into account are the first prerequisite. These ground rules will have to consider the following difficult factors.

The most difficult will be the question of the weight to be given to circumstances surrounding controversial contracts. Many of these contracts have been negotiated under unscrupulous dictators whose only interest was to line their pockets (and those of their relatives and friends), thus selling the birthright of the country at bargain rates and for periods of up to ninety-nine years. Existing constitutional provisions have been flagrantly violated or arbitrarily changed to meet the immediate needs of el jefe—provisions which in many ways have been indicative of the community's sense of justice. Practices of the Mexican dictator, Porfirio Díaz, should have been an obvious danger signal to anyone who wanted to observe it. In some cases constitutional provisions prohibiting further concessions of natural resources are openly ignored and are certain to be a source of trouble at a later date.[81]

Large tracts of land are sometimes purchased at low prices (though perhaps quite reasonable at the time) and are held for possible use in some distant future, being regarded as a reasonable risk.[82] Large parts of a nation's territory are thus withheld from use, a fact which changing circumstances make intolerable in a small and impoverished country.

Expropriation of property has in some cases been the final step in a bitter controversy over labor relations, taxes or profit sharing. At times these demands may have been unreasonable, but certainly in other instances legitimate demands for higher wages or higher taxes have been flatly rejected under the assumption that a government was too weak to enforce its decisions.

Certainly those contracts made under the most superficial cover of legality, a temporary legality created by an unscrupulous dictator's fiat pen, where the terms of the contract are so favorable as to make great risk worthwhile on the part of the investor, are just the kind of risks that can result in losses to those persons who engage in them while causing the least damage to established patterns of social and economic relationships. Losses incurred partly as a result of refusal to accept reasonable burdens and restrictions fall into the same category. The speculative nature of the venture and its effect on the country have to be considered as well. These factors *are* indeed taken into account by foreign offices and claims commissions. But it is done in a completely haphazard and unarticulated fashion, often deliberately disguised in order to preserve the "pure legality" of a position or decision. The legal fiction that damages to the individual are damages to his state have helped to compound the confusion.

Finally there is the matter of the state action that is considered absolutely imperative or perhaps unavoidable. International law is filled with concessions to necessity, the rights and duties of states in time of war being the best example. The decision on a Mexican-American claim (*E. R. Kelley* v. *The United Mexican States*) is illustrative.

As is shown by precedents that have been cited and others that might be mentioned, there is a wide range of defensive measures in time of hostilities. Undoubtedly the justification of such measures must be found in the nature of the emergency in each given case and the methods employed to meet the situation.

With reference to matters more directly connected with actual military affairs there are interesting illustrations of property losses for which those who have suffered such losses have not been considered entitled to compensation.[83]

If war has in the past been an unfortunate but unavoidable fact which international law was forced to take into account, it might well be that the twentieth-century phenomenon of social revolution will now have to be given careful consideration. We refer here, of course, not simply to the period of violence accompanying a social revolution but, rather, to measures applied after a period of violence or even in lieu of such violence.

This was essentially the position taken by the Mexican government with regard to land reform.

The political, social and economic stability and peace of Mexico depends on the land being placed anew in the hands of the country people who work it; therefore, its distribution, which implies the transformation of the country, that is to say, the future of the nation, could not be halted by the impossibility of paying immediately the value of the properties belonging to a small number of foreigners who seek only a lucrative end.[84]

The Bolivians placed the expropriation of the tin mines in the same category, although for different reasons. With notorious meddling by the industries in the internal politics of the state and even opposition to necessary social measures, expropriation was looked on as a necessary corrective for an intolerable political situation.

Every myth or charge against the alien's past or present conduct could not, however, be used to invalidate or reduce his claim. Foreign companies operating in Latin America often face more difficult problems than they face in their home countries because of the uncertainty of the law, arbitrary actions of local officials, inefficiency and often graft. To be effective, new rules of law will have to provide the means for objective evaluation of all these factors. Whether we like it or not, a government that comes into power on the wave of a social revolution simply will not be bound by such contracts as those mentioned.

All this admittedly opens up the very serious possibility that contracts will be made so uncertain as to be useless. But the fact remains that the extreme reactions which the traditional rules are now producing may well make contracts even more uncertain. Furthermore, it is difficult to see why rules which would provide that the factors just discussed should be taken into account would err further in the direction of uncertainty of contract than the traditional rules have erred in the direction of abuse of contract.

Too often the tendency has been to paint the scrupulous investor with the same brush as the unscrupulous one and to treat the matter of compensation as lightly in the one case as in the other. A rule that would take into account the factors we have discussed might well make it possible to make some important distinctions. Had some of these changes been made half a century ago, many of the questionable deals which have become such a fruitful source of conflict might never have been made. Latin American insistence on the doctrine that would make the state responsible only to the point of "equality of treatment" has been in large part a reaction to the failure to adjust the rules to meet some of their well-founded objections. This position will undoubtedly be maintained until some adjustments in the traditional rules are made.

Our discussion thus far may well have created the impression that the solution is largely in the hands of the United States, that is, that a willingness on the part of the latter to accept some changes in the rules and procedures is all that is needed. This assumption is mistaken, to say the least. The problem is seriously complicated by antagonism and resentment from the past, by the impact of social revolutions on

Latin American politics and by the impact of the cold war—matters to be discussed in detail in the next chapter.

The complexity of the problem is manifest in the abortive attempts to form an Inter-American Court of Justice. There can be little doubt that such a court, on which Latin Americans would have a large majority, would be far more sympathetic to their legal doctrines than the usual claims commissions, which have equal representation for each of the parties to a dispute. For this reason the court has received the support of a number of Latin American states and the opposition of the United States.[85] But the situation is further complicated by the fact that other Latin American governments have feared that a court, along with the companion project of an Inter-American Declaration on Human Rights, would provide an opening for intervention into their domestic affairs. The remaining dictators who have come under fire from liberals and reformers throughout Latin America know full well that they would be the first target. Thus, although they might well support such an institution as a means of redefining the rules on responsibility toward aliens, they have even stronger reason to oppose it.

With the cold war making it more and more difficult for the United States to use the traditional weapons of statecraft to secure compliance with its interpretation of the rules, there is also less reason for Latin Americans to seek some compromise solution. The doctrine which would make treatment of aliens entirely a domestic affair, subject only to the qualification of "equality of treatment," seems to serve the interests of some governments better and can gain *de facto* acceptance through lack of effective means of opposing it.

Tensions created by the gulf separating the traditional rules from the social needs of a hemisphere in revolution can be expected to produce unpleasant new explosions in the future. It is, of course, possible that time has already run out and that it is no longer feasible to agree on a workable set of rules. Only an open and serious effort in this direction can give us the answer. One thing seems certain: the task will become more difficult the longer it is evaded.

FOOTNOTES

1. Many of these are discussed in Donald R. Shea, *The Calvo Clause* (Minneapolis, 1955). See also Alwyn V. Freeman, *The International Responsibility of States for Denial of Justice* (New York, 1938; Edwin M. Borchard, *The*

Diplomatic Protection of Citizens Abroad or the Law of International Claims (New York, 1915); Marjorie M. Whitman, *Damages in International Law* (Washington, D.C., 1937–1943); and Frederick Sherwood Dunn, *The Protection of Nationals* (Baltimore, 1932).

2. Edgar Turlington, *Mexico and Her Foreign Creditors* (New York, 1930), pp. 35–37, 116–117, 141.
3. See J. Fred Rippy, *Globe and Hemisphere* (Chicago, 1958), pp. 53 ff.
4. The best statement of this position was made in connection with the Mexican expropriations. See the next section.
5. The best analysis of this aspect of the Mexican social revolution is still Frank Tannenbaum, *Peace by Revolution: An Interpretation of Mexico* (New York, 1933).
6. *Ibid.* See also John L. Johnson, *Political Change in Latin America* (Stanford, Calif., 1958), pp. 128 ff.
7. E. David Cronin, *Josephus Daniels in Mexico* (Madison, 1960), pp. 30 ff. See also B. A. Wortley, "The Mexican Oil Dispute 1938–1946," *Transactions* of the Grotius Society, 1957, vol. 43. p. 16.
8. Wendell C. Gordon, *The Expropriation of Foreign-Owned Property in Mexico* (Washington, D.C., 1941), pp. 42–47.
9. *Ibid.*, pp. 79 ff.; Cronin, *op. cit.*, pp. 154–202.
10. Note of Aug. 3, 1938, reproduced in U.S. Department of State, *Compensation for American-Owned Lands Expropriated in Mexico*, Inter-American Series 16.
11. *The Times* (London), Oct. 24, 1938.
12. Cronin, *op. cit.*, p. 261.
13. *Ibid.*, p. 269.
14. *Ibid.*, pp. 180 ff., 204 ff., 269 ff.
15. *Ibid.*, p. 171.
16. *Ibid.*, p. 179.
17. *Ibid.*, pp. 182 ff.; Howard Cline, *The United States and Mexico* (Cambridge, Mass., 1953), pp. 229–238.
18. Cronin, *op. cit.*, pp. 180, 204.
19. *Ibid.*, p. 270. (Author's Italics)
20. *Ibid.*, p. 270.
21. The settlement is discussed in detail, *ibid.*, chapter 10. See also Cline, *op. cit.*
22. Cronin, *op. cit.*, p. 150.
23. Manuel Galich, *Por que lucha Guatemala?* (Mexico, D.F., 1956), pp. 38–40; Ronald M. Schneider, *Communism in Guatemala* (New York, 1959), p. 48; Elena de la Sochere, "Guatemala: no Communist Beachead," *Monthly Review* (July 1954), p. 105; Theodore Geiger, *Communism Versus Progress in Guatemala* (Washington, D.C., 1953), pp. 44–45.
24. John H. Adler, Eugene R. Schlesinger and Ernest C. Olson, *Public Finance and Economic Development in Guatemala* (Stanford, 1952), p. 124.
25. *Ibid.*, p. 34.
26. Martz, *Central America: The Crisis and The Challenge* (Chapel Hill, N.C., 1959), p. 49.
27. *Ibid.*, p. 52.
28. U.S. Department of State, *Bulletin* (Sept. 14, 1953), pp. 359–360.

29. *Ibid.*, p. 357.
30. See H. L. Saxena, "Revolution and Counter Revolution in Guatemala," *Modern Review* (Sept. 1954), p. 202.
31. *U.S. in World Affairs*, 1953, p. 334; Martz, *op. cit.*, p. 52.
32. Declaración del Ministerio de Relaciones Exteriores de Guatemala, May 21, 1954, reprinted in Guillermo Toriello, *La batalla de Guatemala* (Mexico, D.F., 1955), p. 317.
33. *Hispanic American Report* for Dec. 1954, p. 574, *New York Times*, Dec. 28, 1954.
34. Robert J. Alexander, *The Bolivian National Revolution* (New Brunswick, 1958), p. 95.
35. *Ibid.*, p. 96.
36. *Ibid.*, p. 95.
37. *Lucha Obrera* (La Paz), June 12, 1952.
38. See speech by the Bolivian Ambassador to the United States, reprinted (partially) in Alexander, *op. cit.*, p. 103.
39. See President Paz Estenssoro's Message to Congress, July 1956, excerpted *ibid.*, p. 106.
40. Letter from Marjorie M. Whiteman, Assistant Legal Advisor, U.S. Department of State, June 12, 1961.
41. Alexander, *op. cit.*, pp. 112–113.
42. *Deadline Data on World Affairs*, "Bolivia," Deadline Data, Inc., New York, p. 20.
43. *New York Times*, Oct. 8, 1960.
44. Agrarian Reform Law, published in Cuba, Ministerio de Estado, Departamento de Prensa, *Boletín*, no. 49 (July 20, 1959).
45. *Wall Street Journal*, March 8, 1960; April 6, 1960. On the matter of evaluation of properties see Robert F. Smith, *The United States and Cuba: Business and Diplomacy, 1917–1960* (New York, 1960), pp. 178 ff. He notes that "in a filmed interview a manager of the King Ranch admitted that they were not in a very good position to protest the valuation used by the Cubans: CBS, *Report on Cuba*." See also Samuel Shapiro, "Cuba: A Dissenting Report," *New Republic* (Sept. 19, 1960), p. 12.
46. Second Note (of Oct. 12) to GOC on the Subject of American Properties Affected by the Cuban Agrarian Reform Law, mimeographed.
47. United States Protests Cuban Property Seizures, U.S. Department of State *Press Release*, no. 7, Jan. 11, 1960.
48. Note of Oct. 12, cited.
49. Bonsal to Secretary of State, telegram (mimeographed), July 6, 1960.
50. *Ibid.*
51. United States Protests Cuban Seizure of American Oil Refineries, U.S. Department of State *Press Release*, no. 381, July 5, 1960.
52. *New York Times*, Oct. 26, 1960.
53. Shea, *op. cit.*, pp. 24–32.
54. Wesley L. Gould, *An Introduction to International Law* (New York, 1957), p. 519.
55. *Ibid.*
56. International Commission of Jurists, Public International Law Project, II, reprinted in 22 *AJIL*, Special Supplement (1928), p. 240.

57. Samuel F. Bemis, *The Latin American Policy of the United States* (New York, 1943), p. 251; International Conference of American States, Sixth, *Diario*, pp. 486–505.
58. *Ibid.*, p. 492.
59. International Conference of American States, Sixth, *Actas de las Sesiones Plenarias*, p. 108.
60. *Ibid.*, pp. 109–110.
61. Victor M. Maúrtua, *Intervención, conciliación, arbitraje en las conferencias de La Habana, 1928 y Washington, 1929* (Havana, n.d.), p. 111.
62. *Ibid.*, pp. 111–114.
63. *The International Conferences of American States*, First Supplement, 1933–1940 (Carnegie Endowment for International Peace, Washington, D.C., 1940), pp. 121–123. The United States attached a reservation which in effect stated that it reserved its rights as generally recognized under international law, but Secretary of State Hull gave his assurance that the government of President Roosevelt would respect the principle of non-intervention; *ibid.*
64. *Ibid.*, pp. 165–166. (Author's Italics)
65. Resolution XXXV, *Report of the Delegation of the United States of America to the Inter-American Conference for the Maintenance of Peace* (Washington, D.C., 1937), pp. 27, 232–234.
66. *Diario de Sesiones*, p. 295.
67. Shea, *op. cit.*, pp. 85–86.
68. Article VII.
69. "The Government of the United States cannot accept Article VII relating to diplomatic protection and the exhaustion of local remedies. For its part, the Government of the United States maintains the rules of diplomatic protection, including the rule of exhaustion of local remedies by aliens, as provided by international law." International Conference of American States, Ninth, *Report of the Delegation of the United States of America*, p. 200.
70. Doc. CIJ–39 (English), pp. 10 ff.
71. *Ibid.*, p. 9.
72. Quoted in Shea, *op. cit.*, p. 98.
73. See *Inter-American Juridical Yearbook*, 1952–1954, pp. 63–64; 1955–1957, pp. 97–98; O.A.S. Council, Committee on Legal Affairs, *Proyecto de informe de las Comisión de Asuntos Jurídico-Politicos acerca del resultado de la encuesta sobre el establecimiento de una Corte Interamericana de Justicia* (Feb. 17, 1961), mimeographed; Pan American Union, General Secretariat, *Human Rights in the American States* (1960), pp. 163–166.
74. See the excellent case presented by B. A. Wortley, *Expropriation in Public International Law* (Cambridge, 1959), and his paper, "The Mexican Oil Dispute 1938–1946," *Transactions* of The Grotius Society, 1957, vol. 43, pp. 15–37. See also P. Adriaanse, *Confiscation in Private International Law* (The Hague, 1956); International Law Association, *Report of its Committee on the Juridical Aspect of Nationalization and Foreign Property* (Hamburg Conference, 1960).
75. S. Friedman, *Expropriation in International Law* (London, 1953).
76. Dunn, *op. cit.*, p. 191.
77. *Ibid.*
78. *Ibid.*, p. 201.

79. Reprinted in their article "Responsibility of States for Injuries to the Economic Interests of Aliens," 55, *AJIL* (July 1961), pp. 545–584.
80. See Dunn, *op. cit.*, pp. 113–187.
81. See Rómulo Betancourt, *Venezuela: Política y Petróleo* (Mexico, D.F., 1956), chapters 1–3.
82. See George S. Gibb and Evelyn H. Knoulton, *The Resurgent Years, 1911–1917*, A History of the Standard Oil Company (New York, 1956), p. 383.
83. *25 AJIL* (1931), pp. 388–397, at pp. 391, 396.
84. Note of Aug. 3, 1938, reprinted in U.S. Department of State, *Compensation for American-Owned Lands Expropriated in Mexico*, Inter-American Series 16.
85. *Inter-American Juridical Yearbook*, 1955–1957, p. 98. On traditional United States opposition see Manley O. Hudson, *International Tribunals* (Washington, D.C., 1944), pp. 175–176.

Chapter Four

Intervention, International Law
and the Inter-American System

An old problem in a new context

The growing frequency of armed conflict in the Caribbean and Central America reveals some new and significant aspects of the old problem of intervention. The principle that no state has a right to intervene in the internal affairs of another has been challenged, reassessed and given a number of new interpretations as these conflicts have become the primary concern of the hemisphere.

Two developments which have been proceeding in opposite directions reflect the forces that are placing new strains upon the principle of non-intervention. The first of these is the mounting exactitude and breadth of the non-intervention doctrine itself. It has been applied to collective action as well as to action by individual states; to indirect action, such as diplomatic protests and economic pressure, as well as to more direct action. The second development has been the issuing of declarations on the political, social and economic rights of man. These declarations have been very much concerned with the domestic affairs of states. Although, strictly speaking, they cannot be said to create legal obligations, we shall see that such claims have indeed been made. More important, they are evidence of an attempt to bring in by the back door what has been barred from the front. As such they show the impact of inescapable economic, social and political developments, particularly in Central America and the Caribbean.

The 1940's through the early 1960's have seen the collision of these two developments as (1) the non-intervention doctrine has confronted the facts of intervention, especially in Central America and the Caribbean, (2) movements for social and democratic rights have become messianic and expansive, and (3) the cold war conflict has intruded, offering support to both developments. There is thus an urgent need to reconsider the principle of non-intervention within the context of significant international developments of the past two decades. The failure of juridical thought to keep pace with developments in international politics seems evident.

Virtually all Latin American governments and jurists have continued to deal with the question of intervention almost entirely in the light of what transpired up until the early 1930's, in spite of the fact that in the last two decades there have been ample demonstrations of significant changes in the nature of the problem. Much of the difficulty can be traced to the failure to treat the international politics of Latin America in a completely objective manner. There is a definite tendency among Latin American writers to avoid the unpleasant facts of conflict among the Latin American states, apparently in the name of a sentimental pan-Americanism. Thus the problem of intervention in the Western Hemisphere has been viewed almost exclusively as a struggle in which Latin American states were defending themselves against intervention by the United States (and a few Great Powers in Europe) which sought to protect powerful economic interests and promote imperialistic designs. We can read the great majority of Latin American monographs on intervention as well as textbooks in international law and relations and scarcely be aware that the problem has currently or historically any other aspects.[1] The interventions by Latin American states to be discussed later simply are not mentioned, nor are the early interventions of Brazil and Argentina in Uruguay.

We do not suggest that such one-sided treatment has been an injustice to the United States and Europe. On the contrary, there can be no doubt that the sharp criticisms pointed in this direction were for the most part justified and have on the whole had a beneficial effect on United States policy. What is truly unfortunate is the fact that inquiry into this complex and dangerous problem has been so oversimplified. Concentration on this one aspect of intervention has obscured other equally important aspects. The result has been that when recent and not-so-recent interventions in the Caribbean (mostly by Caribbean governments themselves) began causing troubles in the inter-American system, there had been at best little or no thinking and discussion to provide help in understanding the problem.

At worst, an obsession with "the one great threat" had actually helped to throw the whole question into hopeless confusion. Obsession with "the one great threat" no doubt explains what the Spanish jurist, Barcia Trelles, has criticized as the policy of trying to make an episodic and circumstancial reaction to a single concrete problem into a general and enduring principle of law without considering its harmony with the total legal and political system.[2] In this instance the reaction to United States intervention was a relentless campaign to make an absolute rule of law out of the doctrine of non-intervention. Since the power of the United States in this hemisphere and the possible forms of intervention seemed almost limitless, the prohibition, to be effective, would have had to be absolute and unqualified.

Establishment of the principle of non-intervention

The expression of Latin American resentment to United States intervention reached its peak at the Sixth International Conference of American States, convened at Havana in 1928. Although it was not until the succeeding conference (held in 1933) that the principle of non-intervention was formally written into the Convention on Rights and Duties of States, it is safe to say that the 1928 conference marked the turning point. The proceedings shed a great deal of light on the basic issues involved and provide some clues about why it has been impossible to face the problem squarely in the years since 1928.

In the previous chapter we have referred to the position of the United States at this conference and to the opposing position taken by the majority of Latin American states. But a dilemma which the other delegates chose to ignore was placed squarely before them by Dr. Ferrara of Cuba. He warned that the principle of non-intervention, which was supposed to guarantee freedom and the right of self-determination, might well become the very means by which tyranny would be perpetuated. His eloquent address to the delegates at Havana is as relevant today, in terms of Caribbean problems, as it was then.

The word "Intervention," which for a momentary political impulse is placed on the "Index" in this meeting, has everywhere a glorious past. How much nobility and grandeur there has been in some interventions! If Gladstone, that illustrious English statesman, might live again, he would hardly follow us in a generic repudiation of the word which to him always represented the saving of human lives, the renovation of institutions and the freeing of people from tyranny. The splendid phrases which he pronounced on many occasions, pleading for a civilizing movement against the barbarian, would provide the discourse in reply to the opinions expressed here this afternoon. . . .

These words, then, which today we condemn without distinction, were the longing, the hope and the last recourse for large persecuted groups of humanity. . . .

[If we declare] in absolute terms that intervention is under no circumstances possible, we will be sanctioning all the inhuman acts committed within determined frontiers and, what is worse, we will not be avoiding that which is in the hearts of all to avoid, the onslaught upon the people's rights of sovereignty and independence, which cynical force can always trample upon.[3]

These words were to have an ironic echo more than thirty years later in the less measured words of Fidel Castro and his Minister of Foreign Relations. The principle of non-intervention, they insisted, must not be permitted to serve as a shield behind which dictators such as Trujillo could hide!

But if the Cuban or United States delegations had any ideas concerning the solution of the dilemma which they recognized, they were not presented to the conference. They offered only the remedy of unilateral intervention.

We have also noted in the previous chapter the successful efforts of Latin American states to have the general principle of non-intervention adopted by nearly every inter-American conference since 1933. The most inclusive statement thus far appears in the Charter of the Organization of American States.

No State or group of States has the right to intervene, directly or indirectly, for any reason whatever, in the internal affairs of any other State. The foregoing principle prohibits not only armed force but also any other form of interference or attempted threat against the personality of the State or against its political, economic and cultural elements.[4]

Thus, in their reaction to an immediate problem, Latin Americans have tried to make an ever more absolute rule of law of a doctrine which promised to meet that specific problem. "Inter-American law" was clearly headed down one road, a road which placed greater and greater emphasis on absolute sovereignty.

It is of course true that the procedure of consultation in case of a threat to the peace (under the Treaty of Reciprocal Assistance, 1947, and the Charter of the O.A.S., 1948)* leads in the direction of greater

* Infra, pp. 71–72.

responsibility on the part of all the American states and that this might well lead to *collective* intervention. But it is equally true, as noted by Charles G. Fenwick, that

. . . in none of the applications of the Rio Treaty to date is there anything to suggest that the provisions of the treaty would warrant collective actions beyond the protection of the state against an armed attack or an act of aggression short of an armed attack by the removal of the conditions giving rise to the complaint. Rather the inferences are all the other way.[5]

If evidence is needed on this point, we have only to note the statements by the overwhelming majority of the ministers of foreign relations at their Meeting of Consultation at Santiago de Chile in August 1959.[6] They demonstrate clearly the extent to which non-intervention has been *proclaimed* an absolute unqualifiable principle and the reluctance to qualify it even with respect to collective intervention.

We shall see presently how another development in the inter-American juridical system has been heading in the opposite direction, largely because of revolutionary social and political movements in the area. But first we must ask how well these revolutionary movements have respected the principle of non-intervention.

The principle challenged: totalitarian subversion

Events in South America during and immediately after World War II brought to light some aspects of the problem of intervention not anticipated in 1928. The situation contained many of the elements that were to become more troublesome within a few years: (1) heightened tension between democratic and authoritarian regimes, complicated by growing social and political unrest, (2) a totalitarian ideology which sought to spread its influence by means of clandestine subversive intervention, and (3) growing United States concern for its security. The reputed pro-Nazi leanings of the Ramírez regime, which came to power in Argentina in June 1943, brought it into immediate diplomatic conflict with the United States. In order to strengthen its position against the United States and Brazil, its chief rivals for leadership on the continent, the Ramírez regime and later the Perón regime set about trying to construct a bloc of states which would support Argentina. This led to a series of Argentine interventions and attempts at intervention in Bolivia,[7] Chile,[8] Paraguay[9] and Uruguay.[10] The government of Uruguay was a special target for Argentine efforts, inasmuch as it provided a refuge for numerous Argentine political exiles who were able to carry on their activities only a short distance from home.

In November 1945, the government of Uruguay circulated a note (generally known as the Larreta note) among the other American states.[11] Without being referred to by name, the Argentine government was roundly denounced as a threat to the peace. The note did not point to any specific acts that could be so regarded but insisted rather that such a government was by its very nature contrary to the principles of the inter-American system. "The purest respect for the principles of non-intervention of one state in the affairs of another . . . *does not protect unlimitedly the notorious and repeated violation by any republic of elementary rights of man.*" In the international politics of America, "the parallelism between peace and democracy" should constitute "an indeclinable norm of action."[12] A substantial list of inter-American resolutions and declarations which were supposed to have made democracy and respect for human rights obligatory was cited in support of this.[13] Finally, it was proposed that the American states should consult among themselves about a course of action.

Judged by the standards of most Latin American jurists[14] and statesmen, the Uruguayan reaction to the Argentine situation would in itself be a form of indirect intervention—at least if we are to take seriously the position which denies the right of a state to protest diplomatically concerning unfair treatment of its own citizens by a foreign government. It is somewhat ironic to find Uruguay, one of the most outspoken supporters of this position, submitting a diplomatic protest concerning the treatment offered by a foreign government *not to aliens but to its own citizens, in this case Argentine treatment of Argentine citizens.*

Dr. Rodríguez Larreta's case has been sharply criticized by the Spanish jurist Barcia Trelles.[15] In the latter's opinion, to base such action on the democratic solidarity of America "is not to say much, since those supposed democracies, compared with each other, vary not only in form but in substance as well." Furthermore, he feels that collective action in support of "democracy" would be far more subjective and dangerous than even the Tobar Doctrine.[16] At least that referred to constitutional practices which gave it a measure of objectivity. In his proposal (still according to Barcia) the ideological motives, more than the means of coming to power, are emphasized.

When we read the antecedents invoked by Dr. Rodríguez Larreta in support of the clearly American character of his doctrinal position, we perceive the inherent defect in all dialectical reaction not based upon abstract reasoning. . . . The truth is that the cited doctrine . . . constitutes no more than a dialectical reaction in the face of a concrete fact, in this case the Argentine fact.[17]

Barcia's criticism would seem to be justified insofar as it refers to the Uruguayan claim that collective intervention is justified under *existing* international law. Just as the doctrine of absolute non-intervention was proclaimed in the face of one specific threat, United States intervention, so the doctrine of a right of collective intervention in the name of democracy is proclaimed as a principle of law in the face of another threat, Argentina. As already pointed out, Barcia's assertion that the Larreta note itself was a form of indirect intervention is not without foundation.

But it is important to note that Dr. Rodríguez Larreta's proposals were not quite this rigid. He was also proposing consultation among the American states on the "parallelism between peace and democracy."[18] This would at least leave open the question whether American states were legally obliged to practice democracy.

Only four states agreed with the Uruguayan position[19] and, of these four, the United States seemed to support only the idea of consultation on the parallelism between peace and democracy. Most of the replies clearly showed a strong reluctance to compromise *in any way* the principle of non-intervention. El Salvador, for example, rejected flatly the idea that the principle referred only to unilateral intervention. "The same reason which exists for declaring inadmissible the intervention of one, holds for not accepting the intervention of many and if the intervention of one constitutes a serious danger to the peace, that of the many could convert the continent into a Camp of Agramonte."[20]

The principle challenged: social revolution and cold war

Two principal factors account for the recent outburst of interventionist policies in the Caribbean.

1. Although no precise date can be set, during the 1930's movements began developing throughout Latin America demanding fundamental changes not only in political institutions but in the structure of society as well. Sometimes these movements continued to emphasize

political democracy and respect for human rights. But, more and more, the emphasis was placed on freeing the downtrodden masses from their economic and social bondage rather than on the means for doing so, although lip service was paid to "true democracy," "social democracy" or "meaningful democracy." The distinctive feature of all these movements, in contrast to the many earlier "revolutions," was the insistence on fundamental changes which would root out the old pattern of oligarchic and foreign control. Peru's *Apra*, Venezuela's *Acción Democrática*, Guatemala's assortment of "Revolutionary" parties (after 1945) and Bolivia's *Movimiento Nacional Revolucionario* represented the worst of evils to conservatives in these countries.

This fact made the struggles for control of governments something quite different from the traditional rivalry among factions within the old oligarchy and the army, which in the past had seldom threatened the established economic and social order. It meant that future political struggles would be more and more the product and the producer of messianic zeal and that greater and greater numbers of people would come to feel a real stake in them. World War II, with the Western Allies' condemnation of dictatorship and promises of "a better world for all," gave a fillip to these tensions, and cold war propaganda, which followed almost immediately, continued the process by showing how abundant life could be under the political and economic systems advocated by the two major contenders. In an already unstable area such developments were certain to have an impact, especially when added to a second factor.

2. Certain areas of Latin America (the Caribbean and Central America being the most notable) have always had large floating populations of refugees from some neighboring political regime. Usually their major interest has been in plotting the overthrow of the regime from which they had recently fled, and therefore they have always been a factor of instability. As long as conflicts within these states involved only factions within the ruling oligarchy and the army, however, the refugee problem could be kept under control. The 1928 Convention on Rights and Duties of States in Time of Civil Strife[21] served remarkably well under these conditions.

But where a new regime has come to power promising to sweep away the old order, to lift the underprivileged masses from their present state of servitude and to "respect the sovereignty of the people," it will probably treat the refugee problem quite differently. Given the presence of refugees from some neighboring dictatorial regime (and there are certain to be some), and given the strong popular feelings released by a recent overthrow of dictatorship in the host state, it is most unlikely that a government would risk unpopular measures intended to prevent them from plotting against a regime which is universally detested. Popular enthusiasm, messianic complexes of popular leaders and the expediency of appealing to a popular revolutionary mood offer irresistible temptations for governments to look the other way or even offer support to plotting refugees.

The reaction of dictatorial regimes is not difficult to surmise. They too can permit refugees to plot the overthrow of the regime that threw them out of power, and if necessary they can assist them. This is not to say that plots to overthrow a regime are always a *reaction* on the part of a dictatorship to a process started by zealous revolutionary neighbors. In politics of this sort it is usually impossible to determine who sets the process in motion. It is enough to know that, for the reasons cited, unstable political regimes have found it "necessary" to conspire or at least permit conspiracies on their territory against neighboring regimes.

The growing danger of conflict within the hemisphere as well as threats from extracontinental sources stimulated efforts to form a more effective security system. In 1947, representatives of the American states met at Rio de Janeiro to complete a mutual security system which had already been evolving through various resolutions and declarations. The Inter-American Treaty of Reciprocal Assistance which the conference produced was certainly one of the more notable achievements of American cooperation up until that time.

Two categories of situations and responses envisaged in the treaty are most important for our purposes. First, in the event of an armed attack against the territory of an American state within this hemisphere, the contracting parties agree to offer individually such assistance as they deem advisable.[22] Meanwhile, the Organ of Consultation (the Meeting of the Ministers of Foreign Affairs, or, provisionally, the Council of the O.A.S.) of the Inter-American System is to meet and determine what measures of a collective character must be taken.[23]

Second, if there is a threat to the sovereignty or territory of an American state which is not an armed attack or if there is "any other fact or situation that might endanger the peace of America," the Organ of Consultation will also meet to determine what measures must be taken.[24] In both instances (an armed attack or any threat short of that) the measures will be decided on by a two-thirds majority. Parties to a dispute may not participate in the voting.[25] Both cases cover attacks or threats from an American state as well as from extracontinental powers.[26] All signatories are bound to carry out a decision, except when the use of armed force is prescribed. Other measures (which would be obligatory) are specified: recall of chiefs of diplomatic missions; breaking of diplomatic relations; breaking of consular relations; partial or complete interruption of economic relations or of rail, sea, air and other communications.[27]

The situation in the Caribbean soon tested the machinery that had been set up at Rio. A brief look at two of the more serious incidents will illustrate the impact of the movements just described.[28]

On December 11, 1948, the Costa Rican Ambassador in Washington informed the Council of the O.A.S. that "the territory of Costa Rica had been invaded by armed forces proceeding from Nicaragua" and invoked the Inter-American Treaty of Reciprocal Assistance.[29] After due investigation, a special committee of the Council reported that "there is not the slightest doubt of the failure of the Nicaraguan Government to take adequate measures to prevent revolutionary activities directed against a neighboring and friendly country from being carried out." But the guilt was not entirely on one side. The committee also found that "for many months before the invasion the so-called Legion of the Caribbean, or Caribbean Legion, with material and moral help from the Costa Rican Government, enjoyed official sympathy and facilities for carrying out its program and activities, both of which, according to general opinion in the Caribbean area, were designed to overthrow certain governments, among them the present regime in Nicaragua." The usual plea that difficult border areas make it virtually impossible to prevent such activities cannot be sustained in this case. The committee was very explicit in pointing out that both governments *could* and *should* have taken adequate measures.[30]

By 1950, the germ of intervention and counter-intervention had spread throughout the Caribbean and Central America. As a result of complaints by the government of Haiti, the special committee of investigation found evidence which implicated Cuba, the Dominican Republic, Guatemala and Costa Rica. It found, first of all, that the Dominican Republic had permitted refugees to carry on, in Dominican territory, "activities designed to disturb the internal peace of Haiti." It also found "that certain Dominican officials not only tolerated the activities of [a conspirator against the Haitian government] but aided him in the November-December conspiracy."[31]

More significant, however, is the fact that this incident was related to other conspiracies going back a number of years.

It is well known that during the first half of 1947 the activities of conspirators who were intending to invade the Dominican Republic were initiated in Cuba. In Habana and at other points in Cuba, more than 1000 men were gathered together and trained, and made ready for the use of armed force.

Information appearing in the Press shows that public recruiting took place in Cuban territory for the purpose of increasing the expeditionary forces.

The expeditionary forces included citizens of many nationalities, many of whom came to Cuba individually or in groups from their countries of residence or origin, and their arrival could not have taken place unknown to the authorities.

Finally, all of the man power and war materials that had been dispersed over different parts of Cuba, were concentrated at Cayo Confites. The action preceding the concentration at that point, and the presence of an expeditionary army there could not have been accomplished without full knowledge on the part of Cuban civil and military authorities, a fact that was confirmed by ex-President Grau San Martín in the declaration published by the review "Bohemia" in its issue of June 26, 1949.[32]

The government of Guatemala had also been involved in this affair. The committee found "that Guatemalan authorities facilitated and permitted continuous and illegal activities as regards traffic in arms and passage of planes" delivering armaments. "It is likewise a fact," the committee concluded, that revolutionary leaders and many others connected with these illicit activities "enjoyed privileges and facilities that were helpful in the preparation of the Luperon attack."[33]

These conflicts have been further complicated by the intrusion of the cold war into the area. That one of the key elements of Soviet foreign policy is intervention through subversion is too well known to need further discussion here. When this happens, or when the United States is convinced that it has happened, in the Western Hemisphere, it becomes a matter of concern to Washington. With its security threatened (or when it is convinced that it is) the United States will seek ways of circumventing the principle of non-intervention, just as the Caribbean and Central American governments have done.

Secretary Dulles' maneuvers at the Tenth Inter-American Conference in 1954 are almost universally regarded in Latin America as a prime example of intervention. The product of these maneuvers was the Declaration of Solidarity for the Preservation of the Political Integrity of the American States Against the Intervention of International Communism. It declared

. . . that the domination or control of the political institutions of any American State by the international communist movement . . . would constitute a threat to the sovereignty and political independence of the

American States, endangering the peace of America, and would call for a Meeting of Consultation to consider the adoption of appropriate action in accordance with existing treaties.[34]

There was little doubt at Caracas that Secretary Dulles had the Guatemalan government in mind, although his resolution would provide the basis for action should similar threats arise in other places in the hemisphere. But any attempt to extend the scope beyond the specific threat which the United States had in mind was doomed to failure. Even the diplomatic language of the report of the United States delegation cannot obscure this fact.

Several of the amendments proposed reflected a desire among various delegations to give greater attention to the promotion of human rights, the effective exercise of representative democracy, and the development of economic and social well-being as means for combating communism. Recognizing the desirability of reaffirming these traditional concepts but considering it inadvisable to expand the scope of the proposed resolution to accomplish this purpose, the Committee decided to incorporate the amendments in a separate resolution entitled the "Declaration of Caracas" (XCV). The Panamanian amendment relating to the abolition of racial discrimination as a means of fighting communism was also made the subject of a separate resolution (XCIV).[35]

But neither the resolution against racial discrimination nor the resolution on human rights and the development of economic and social well-being calls for anything like a meeting of consultation to make it effective.[36] The United States could hardly risk such action with regard to the former (racial discrimination). On the other hand, we need have little doubt what would have happened to our strongest supporters—Venezuela (then under the Pérez Jiménez dictatorship), the Dominican Republic (then under Trujillo), Cuba (then under Batista) and Peru (then under the Odría dictatorship)[37]—if the resolution on human rights had been included.

It is of course true that the "existing treaties" referred to in the Dulles resolution say nothing about collective action in support of democracy or human rights.[38] Thus the resolution justified the proposed action on the assumption that Communist domination of the political institutions of any American state would endanger the peace and security of the hemisphere. But some Latin American delegates were careful to point out that failure to practice democracy, protect human rights and give adequate attention to economic and social well-being all provided the environment in which Communism would grow.[39] Thus their amendments were also based on the security of the hemisphere, although they wanted to begin one step further back. Mr. Dulles left the conference after gaining approval of his project, and the other resolutions were relegated to the status of pious pronouncements.

The way was now open for calling a Meeting of Consultation, and such a meeting was in fact set for July 7, 1954 in order to consider the danger posed by the international Communist movement in Guatemala.[40] Before the appointed date, however, the government of Guatemala was overthrown and, the immediate cause for alarm being removed, the meeting was postponed *sine die*.[41]

But only the most superficial understanding of the nature of the Communist movement could permit the assumption that the threat,* if it had existed in the first place, had been removed by a mere change in government. The Honduran motion, seconded by the United States, that the meeting be postponed *sine die* raised many questions indeed. Perón's Argentina (now on the side of *los ángeles*) assured everyone that it too was anti-Communist but insisted that the Guatemelan affair had only been the beginning of armed interventions and that it was deeply concerned with such affairs. In the light of the serious accusations made by the late Guatemalan government, the Argentine representative felt that those who had been implicated would welcome a chance to confirm their denials.[42] But the brand of intervention that the United States feared (Communist intervention) had apparently been dealt with, and it was not in the least interested in pushing the question beyond this point.

The successful revolutions against oppressive dictatorships in Venezuela in 1958 and Cuba in early 1959 were the catalyst for a new wave of interventions. Hardly a week passed throughout the year without some complaint. Although it is a fact that numerous expeditions were launched to overthrow several of the governments in the area, the extent to which they were aided by active or passive government support cannot be determined until reports of objective investigations are available. Dr. Castro's statement shortly after assuming power in Cuba was scarcely calculated to ease the tension: "One must feel solidarity with all the exiles of the various dictatorships of Trujillo, Somoza and Paraguay which yet remain in America and I will say that they can count on my aid and sympathy."[43] Although in later statements he pledged himself to abide by the principle of non-intervention,[44] this

* Either the more specific threat of "Guatemalan Communism" or the general threat of Communism in the hemisphere.

revision inspired little confidence as far as the rest of the Caribbean area was concerned.

In this atmosphere the Meeting of Consultation of Ministers of Foreign Affairs of the American States met in Santiago de Chile, August 12–18, thirty-one years after the eventful meeting at Havana. In addition to the fact that both conferences met in the midst of hotly debated interventions (the latter being called for this specific reason), there are some remarkable similarities. Cuba, the Dominican Republic and Nicaragua were at the center of the controversy in both cases, but for quite different reasons. More significant is the fact that many of the same arguments in support of intervention were repeated at Santiago, almost as if one conference had been but a second session of the other.

The Venezuelan Minister declared that "there is a danger that too much emphasis may be given to the question of non-intervention while overlooking the importance of liberty and self-determination for the development of the hemisphere."[45] He noted also that "Napoleon in Europe and Bolívar in America extended the principle of liberty with support of arms. The O.A.S. must consolidate the inter-American system or let it deteriorate."[46] Both Cuba and Venezuela called for a *cordón sanitario* around dictatorial regimes.[47]

It is of course true that they did speak of *collective* intervention from time to time. But it is also true that, in the absence of agreement on collective intervention, they strongly opposed a permanent inter-American committee of vigilance to prevent unilateral intervention throughout the hemisphere.[48] The Cuban Minister insisted that such a committee would itself violate the sovereignty which it sought to protect, and his counterpart in Venezuela said that it would only serve as a shield for dictators.

Even Dr. Ferrara's eloquent reference (Havana, 1928) to the nobility of interventions which had freed Cuba from the yoke of Spain found an ironic sequel in the Dominican Minister's remarks. He assured the Cuban Minister that the only expedition ever to leave his country bound for Cuba was the one that brought José Martí.[49]

There were some interesting contrasts in the conferences as well. Although the ghost of 1928 was very much present and accounted for the reaction of most delegations to any suggestion of collective intervention, the United States was not the target for all complaints as she had been thirty-one years earlier. A second difference is the fact that at the 1928 conference intervention was discussed frankly and openly. Whatever else is said about the interventions of the late nineteenth and early twentieth century, they were frankly admitted and could be identified and discussed for what they were. The interventions of the past two decades, on the contrary, are indignantly denied by those who perpetrate them, this in the face of clear evidence presented by the O.A.S. The problem is thereby made that much more difficult to deal with.

Finally, and perhaps it is the most significant difference, in 1959 there was at least more discussion of international and organizational responsibility. As mentioned earlier, those who called for collective intervention clearly had specific governments in mind, and when it appeared that collective intervention might be treated in more abstract terms, there was less interest. But this conference did at least get beyond the usual rigid pronouncements of the doctrine of non-intervention. It entrusted the Inter-American Peace Committee with the study of three related questions: (a) "methods and procedures to prevent any activities from abroad designed to overthrow established governments or provoke instances of intervention," (b) "the relationship between violation of human rights or the nonexistence of representative democracy, on the one hand, and the political tensions that affect the peace of the hemisphere, on the other," and (c) "the relationship between economic under-development and political instability."[50]

The Inter-American Juridical Committee promptly prepared a *Study on the Juridical Relations between the Respect for Human Rights and the Exercise of Democracy*. In this report a majority of the delegates felt that there was not, at the present time, any legal basis in the Charter of the O.A.S. or elsewhere for organization action "in defense of democracy, for its maintenance, or for its restoration."[51] But events soon moved ahead of legal doctrine.

The Sixth Meeting of Consultation of the Ministers of Foreign Affairs was convened in August 1960 at San José, Costa Rica. It met in response to Venezuelan charges that the Dominican Republic had been involved in the efforts of certain Venezuelans to assassinate President Rómulo Betancourt and was therefore guilty of aggression and of intervention in Venezuelan affairs. Upon substantiation of the facts by a committee appointed by the O.A.S. Council, the meeting voted to condemn the action of the Dominican Republic and recommended that all O.A.S. members break diplomatic relations with the Trujillo regime and observe a strict arms embargo.[52]

Although, strictly speaking, the action was taken in response to Dominican aggression, there is much to suggest that the nature of the Trujillo regime and the desire to bring about its downfall played an important part in the decision. Secretary of State Herter noted, for example, that "these measures are intended to contribute to the establishment there of a government which will be both representative and responsive to its obligations within the inter-American system."[53] In the same vein, the Venezuelan Foreign Minister declared that "it has been noted that the treaty [Rio Treaty] was intended by the United States to intervene in the life of Latin American nations, but it is being used for the first time against a ferocious dictatorship."[54] All this was further suggested by a subsequent decision of the Council of the O.A.S. calling for economic sanctions even though, as the six abstainers pointed out, there had been no further acts of aggression to justify this decision.[55]

Two developments connected with this meeting are especially revealing. First, the United States supported the anti-Trujillo resolution. Second, on the eve of our delegation's departure for San José, President Eisenhower asked Congress for a commitment to spend some $600,000,000 in economic assistance to Latin American countries.[56] Latin Americans were perhaps not far wrong in quipping that Fidel Castro could be thanked for this. The United States was indeed anxious to obtain a strong resolution against the Castro government on the same grounds that it had advanced for the Guatemalan resolution at Caracas. This was the purpose of the Seventh Meeting of the foreign ministers, which convened immediately after passing the anti-Trujillo resolution.

To some Latin Americans the results of the Seventh Meeting must have carried an element of retributive justice. At Caracas the Latin Americans had gone along with Dulles, only to be let down when economic problems and problems of dictatorship came up for discussion. At San José the United States had committed itself on economic assistance and on Trujillo, only to find that a very mild and uncertain resolution against Castro was the best that it could obtain. Without any specific reference to Cuba, it merely condemned intervention by any extracontinental power in the affairs of the American republics and rejected "attempts of the Sino-Soviet powers to make use of the political, economic or social situation of any American state."[57]

The most recent chapter in this complicated episode was added when it became known that the United States government had been assisting Cuban refugees in their preparations for an invasion of Cuba. Arms, money, training and even transport facilities had apparently been given. The exact amount of assistance may never be known, but assuredly it was enough to establish beyond all doubt that the United States would react in the same way that Caribbean and Central American governments have done whenever it felt its security threatened. As if to emphasize this, President Kennedy declared only a few days after the fiasco that "if the nations of this hemisphere should fail to meet their commitments against outside communist penetration . . . this Government will not hesitate in meeting its primary obligations."[58],*

The principle challenged: protection of human rights

Although the revolutionary movements mentioned have contributed to governmental action clearly contrary to the principle of non-intervention, they have also been a factor in a less violent development, the fruits of which are being used to attack on legal grounds the absolute interpretation of the principle. The demands behind these revolutionary movements began to find their way into the inter-American conferences, where all the American states were asked to declare themselves in support of democratic government and constitutional guarantees of certain basic human rights.

Sometimes these demands for democratic government and human rights represented an honest desire on the part of a government to see these principles written into a charter. At other times it was part of a propaganda battle to embarrass and weaken the position of a neighboring (dictatorial) regime. At still others it no doubt represented a cynical and opportunistic attitude on the part of a dictatorial regime desiring to pay lip service to ideals which it recognized as popular at home and abroad.

Whatever the motives, inter-American declarations and resolutions

* In January of 1962 the American ministers of foreign affairs met at Punta del Este, Uruguay, to consider the threat presented by Sino-Soviet influence in Cuba. Twenty states agreed (Cuba disagreed) "that adherence by any member of the Organization of American States to Marxism-Leninism is incompatible with the inter-American system and that alignment of such government with the Communist bloc breaks the unity and solidarity of the hemisphere" and "that the present Government of Cuba, which has officially identified itself as a Marxist-Leninist government is incompatible with the principles and objectives of the inter-American system." Fourteen states resolved "that this incompatibility excludes the present government of Cuba from participation in the inter-American system." Argentina, Bolivia, Brazil, Chile, Ecuador and Mexico abstained; Cuba voted no. See Final Act of the Eighth Meeting of Consultation of the Ministers of Foreign Affairs of the American States, January 1962.

began to refer to liberty and democracy not only as ideals but as concepts already put into practice. Thus resolution XVII of the Inter-American Conference for the Maintenance of Peace, held at Buenos Aires in 1936, declared "that the American Nations, true to their republican institutions, proclaim their absolute juridical liberty, their unqualified respect for their respective sovereignties and the existence of a common democracy throughout America." The delegates made this declaration "having considered: That they have a common likeness in their democratic form of government and their common ideals of peace and justice."[59] Each succeeding conference and meeting has reiterated similar declarations, all of which were about equally remote from the facts. The preamble to the Charter of the O.A.S. states "that the true significance of American solidarity and good neighborliness can only mean the consolidation on this continent, within the framework of democratic institutions, of a system of individual liberty and social justice based on respect for the essential rights of man." More recently, the Declaration of Santiago de Chile declares that "the principle of the rule of law should be assured by the separation of powers," that "the governments of the American republics should be derived from free elections," and that "human rights . . . should be protected by effective judicial procedures."[60]

Although such documents cannot be considered statements of international law even among the American states, they do demonstrate a growing desire to make it obligatory for each state to provide certain constitutional guarantees of basic human rights. It means at least that "the ground has been plowed, and in some future inter-American conference there may arise the feeling that the seeds sown at Bogotá have matured. These freedoms and human rights will then be so firmly entrenched in the thinking of the Americas that deviation from them cannot be tolerated."[61]

No conference has yet come close to doing this, but the number of states which have claimed individually that the documents have legal force has been increasing. We have already noted that in 1945 the government of Uruguay took this position and was supported by Guatemala, Panama and Venezuela. In its reply the government of Guatemala observed that the Uruguayan note "supported with the full force of the democratic tradition of Uruguay, the position which the Guatemalan delegation, responding to the general feeling of the Revolutionary Government and people of this republic, had the honor to present . . . at the Conference of Chapultepec."[62]

In view of the position which it took at the Meeting of Consultation at Santiago de Chile, the government of Cuba appeared to have added itself to this list (at least temporarily). But at the same meeting Guatemala would seem to have returned to a more conservative position (temporarily, perhaps) in favoring only a meeting to prepare a convention for sanctions against aggression.[63] In January of 1960 the President of Brazil offered very qualified support,[64] and in February Venezuela again demanded that the O.A.S. intervene to protect human rights in the Dominican Republic.[65]

Thus, although these documents do represent popular aspirations, they have in recent years been equally important in other respects. They have provided a convenient justification and a convenient norm for denouncing a neighboring regime, either when the latter is actually considered a threat to the security of the government issuing the denunciation or when such denunciation serves the interest of domestic politics. We have seen that they provide a convenient justification for demanding collective intervention and even for hinting at a right of unilateral intervention. In short, they are used as a type of "legal" weapon for attacking the absolute interpretation of the principle of non-intervention, especially in response to immediate political or security requirements. As this tendency becomes more pronounced and thereby moves farther and farther away from the principle of non-intervention, the tension between the two can only become more serious. This is the problem now facing the inter-American system.

The dilemma of a troubled hemisphere

There can be no doubt that the principle of non-intervention is still generally regarded as fundamental to the inter-American system, that American governments do regard it as a rule of law, and that they are well aware of breaking the law when they resort to intervention. Yet the fact remains that in the past two decades Central America and the Caribbean have probably seen more cases of intervention than any other area of the world outside the Soviet sphere. Furthermore, few if any states in the area can honestly plead innocence.

When a government feels threatened by a neighboring regime with an antagonistic ideological and political orientation (or when its domestic and foreign interests make it convenient to picture such a regime as a threat), there is a growing tendency to insist on a right of collective intervention. But almost invariably the intervention called for is directed at a specific regime. Thus Uruguay called for intervention against Nazi-type dictatorships, the United States called for intervention against Communist-dominated regimes, and Venezuela and Cuba have called for a *cordón sanitario* around the Trujillo, Somoza and Paraguayan regimes. Any proposal to think of intervention in more abstract terms has very little appeal. Each government, of course, fears that some feature of its own political, economic or social system will be grounds for embarrassing discussion and investigation, if not intervention. The United States has its racial problems, complicated by the federal system, and there are few Latin American states whose political system would not offer grounds for complaint.

By no means the least cause for concern is the old problem of "denial of justice" to aliens.[66] Conflicts over the treatment of United States private investments throughout Latin America are still far from being a thing of the past, and the awareness of this fact brings back the ghost of 1928. Any reference to collective intervention revives the fear of United States intervention under a different name. Raul Roa, Cuban Minister of Foreign Relations, was only expressing without the usual tact what most delegations at Santiago probably feared when he declared that a Caribbean Commission would be only a tool of United States intervention.[67]

To this must be added the concern aroused by the Guatemalan cases. The United States, unlike Latin American states which had earlier proposed collective intervention, was able to force its resolution through in the face of reluctant partners. But there can be little doubt that it was United States power rather than genuine agreement which was responsible for approval. Sydney Gruson described it accurately in *The New York Times.*

> Señor Toriello [Guatemalan Minister of Foreign Relations] said many nasty things about the United States that virtually all Latin Americans believe. They were willing to applaud him since it cost them nothing. But not many were willing to vote against the United States when they might have to get up later in the Conference and ask for economic aid. In the committee vote, only Mexico, Uruguay and Argentina sided with Guatemala.[68]

It may well be that the "success" of the United States in gaining the necessary votes for its declaration has been offset by the resentment created. By calling back the ghost of 1928, it has helped to make the problem that much more difficult to deal with. The full impact of the ill-fated Cuban venture remains to be seen.

Yet it must be remembered that all this came about as a result of what the United States, rightly or wrongly, regarded as a requirement of continental security, raising the question whether a rule of law intended to provide protection against a democratic power with limited imperialistic ambitions is adequate in the face of a totalitarian power with imperialistic ambitions on a global scale. The voices insisting that the United States cannot counter Soviet intervention with a policy of scrupulous non-intervention will undoubtedly increase if such crises become more frequent. On the other hand, Latin Americans are justifiably concerned that there will be more cases similar to those of Guatemala and Cuba. To most of them the only hope seems to rest in a stronger statement of the principle of non-intervention.

But it is as useless to outlaw intervention without providing a satisfactory substitute as it was to outlaw war when no satisfactory substitute was available. When the apparent "necessity" of intervention appears to outweigh any long-term advantages of preserving the principle of non-intervention, states will resort to the former. This holds true for small powers as well as great powers, and the record of the past two decades shows an increasing number of apparent "necessities."

The problem of intervention should be, and indeed has been, a cause for sober concern on the part of jurists and statesmen in this hemisphere. Dr. Ferrara's plea before the Sixth International Conference of American States, that absolute non-intervention in the name of liberty and self-determination of peoples could defeat the very ideals it sought to protect, has been forcefully vindicated. Now it might be asked whether refusal to compromise on the principle of absolute non-intervention will not threaten the very principle itself. It can of course continue to be honored in countless declarations and protests, but if it does not square with the hard facts of international politics, that will be the extent of its honor. It will require more than pronouncements against intervention and a periodic parading of the ghost of 1928. It will also require much less opportunism on the part of the United States than that shown at the Caracas conference and in events thereafter.

To some it appeared that at Caracas and San José Latin Americans were dragging their feet in recognizing the legitimate security interests of the United States. But to many others, Secretary Dulles' failure to show equal interest in Latin American attempts to relate hemisphere security to problems of economic and social well-being appeared fully as shortsighted. As long as the question of intervention continues to be dealt with exclusively in response to some specific and immediate threat facing a state or a group of states, the real problem tends to remain untouched. The severe limitation of collective intervention, the fact that attempts to enforce democracy and respect for human rights would probably create as many problems as they would solve, is too often brushed aside. The same thing can be said concerning attempts to prevent Communist subversion.

Ten years ago a study dealing with some of these same problems suggested that procedures to prevent acts of aggression in this hemisphere would have to be "supplemented not only by investigation of the status of democratic development, but by well-planned, systematic, intensive effort to ameliorate or remove the basic causes of inter-American friction."[69] Although the past ten years have seen considerably more effort in this direction, it is doubtful whether it could be called "well-planned," "systematic" or "intensive." New and more positive measures were promised by the United States at the August 1961 meeting of the Inter-American Economic and Social Council in Punta del Este, Uruguay. Secretary of the Treasury Douglas Dillon promised long-term loans of up to fifty years and foresaw an inflow of foreign capital for Latin America of up to twenty billion dollars during the next decade, *mostly from public sources.*[70]

The success of this program, called the Alliance for Progress, will depend in large part on the willingness and ability of Latin American governments to institute and sustain fundamental social and economic reforms often opposed by powerful conservatives. One of the difficult questions now confronting the United States is how on the one hand to make the Alliance for Progress effective and on the other to avoid charges of intervention in the internal affairs of the Latin American republics. There will be ample opportunity for some Latin Americans to shout "intervention" if assistance is refused to reactionary, dictatorial governments and to shout "friend of dictatorships" if such assistance is given.

Thus *absolute* non-intervention becomes an impossible and utopian objective insofar as the United States is concerned. The political and economic power of the United States is so great that anything it *does* or *does not do* in relation to another American republic influences the political affairs of that republic. Responsible persons in the United States and Latin America will have to face the fact that it will be a matter of deciding *how* and *with what objective* to intervene rather than taking an utterly impossible and unrealistic "non-intervention" position. Finally, it is only fair to point out that most Latin American critics of United States intervention, while speaking in terms of intervention *generally*, more often than not have in mind those cases of "intervention for the wrong reasons," that is, intervention in support of a detested dictator or in support of United States investors.

FOOTNOTES

1. See, for example, the following monographs: Enrique Aguirre y F. Harris, *La no intervención y la quiebra de la soberania nacional* (Mexico, 1946); Xavier Terrazas Sanchez, *El princípio de la no intervención* (Mexico, 1955); Ismael Augusto Rueda Villarreal, *La no intervención en el derecho internacional americano* (Mexico, 1948); Ramon López Jiménez, *El princípio de no intervención en América y la nota Uruguaya* (Buenos Aires, 1947); Manuel Guzman Vial, *La intervención y la no intervención* (Santiago de Chile, 1948); Isidro Fabela, *Intervención* (Mexico, 1959); Bernardo Jiménez Montellano, *Fundamentos jurídicos de la solidaridad americana* (Mexico, 1948). See also the following textbooks on international law: Luicio Moreno Quintana y Carlos Bollini Shaw, *Derecho internacional público* (Buenos Aires, 1950), pp. 126–136; Manuel J. Sierra, *Tratado de derecho internacional público* (segunda edición, Mexico, 1955), pp. 171–177; Alfred Cook Arango, *Derecho internacional público contemporaneo* (segunda edición, Bogotá, 1955), p. 218 refers at least to Nicaraguan interventions in Costa Rica; Alberto Avellan Vite, *Anotaciones der derecho internacional público* (segunda edición, Guayaquil, 1956), pp. 160–163, 449–460. Even Alberto Ulloa's superb text, 4th ed., Madrid, 1957, vol. I, deals lightly with a few Caribbean interventions as "accusations"; see p. 331.
2. Camilo Barcia Trelles, *Estudios de política internacional y derecho de gentes* (Madrid, 1949), pp. 87–136.
3. *Diario*, p. 503.
4. Article 15.
5. *53 AJIL* (Oct. 1959), p. 875.
6. *Infra*, p. 76. By far the best coverage of this meeting will be found in *La Prensa* of Lima and *La Prensa* of Buenos Aires, Aug. 18–19, 1949.
7. George I. Blanksten, *Perón's Argentina* (Chicago, 1953), pp. 402–403. Robert J. Alexander, *The Perón Era* (New York, 1951), p. 197.
8. *Ibid.*, p. 195.
9. Alexander, *op. cit.*, p. 197.
10. *Ibid.* In 1949, ex-President Rómulo Betancourt of Venezuela filed charges before the United Nations alleging that the Argentine Military Attaché in Caracas had played a prominent part in the overthrow of the democratically elected government of Venezuela. He said, "there is in America a 'Reactionary International' headed by Argentina and General Perón," *ibid.*, p. 196.
11. Uruguay, Ministerio de Relaciones Exteriores, *Paralelismo entre la democracia y la paz. Protección internacional de los derechos del hombre. Acción colectiva en defensa de esos princípios* (Montevideo, 1946), pp. 7–12.
12. *Ibid.*
13. *Ibid.* It was noted, for example, that at the Buenos Aires conference, 1936, "the existence of a democratic solidarity in America was proclaimed." Resolu-

tion XXII of the Panama conference, 1939, resolved that "more than once the American republics have affirmed their adhesion to the democratic ideal which prevails in this hemisphere; that this ideal could be endangered by action of foreign ideologies inspired by principles diametrically opposed and that it is opportune, consequently, to guard against their intangibility through adopton of appropriate measures." Resolution VIII of the Havana conference, 1940, referred to the "propagation of doctrines tending to endanger the common ideal of inter-American democracy." In Resolution VII of the Mexico City conference, 1945, the parties affirmed "their adhesion to the democratic ideal."

14. See, for example, Maúrtua, "La Declaración sobre Derechos y Deberes de los Estados en las Naciones Unidos." *Revista Peruana de Derecho Internacional*, IX (1949), pp. 227–245, and *supra*, pp. 50 ff.

15. Barcia Trelles, *op. cit.*

16. The Tobar Doctrine called for the withholding of recognition of any government which might come into existence by revolutionary means.

17. Barcia Trelles, *op. cit.*, p. 135.

18. Uruguay, Ministerio de Relaciones Exteriores, *op. cit.*, p. 5.

19. Replies reprinted *ibid.*, pp. 12 ff. Costa Rica gave a very qualified approval.

20. *Ibid.*

21. Signed at Havana, 1928. Provides that the contracting parties must use all means at their disposal to prevent nationals as well as aliens within their territory from participating in civil strife in another American state by gathering elements for it, or from crossing the boundary or sailing from their territory for purposes of starting or promoting such strife. Each party is called upon to disarm and intern rebel forces entering its territory, forbid traffic in arms (except with the recognized government of the country) when the belligerency of the rebels has not been recognized, and prevent the arming or equipping of any vessel intended to operate in favor of the rebellion.

22. Article 3.

23. Article 6.

24. *Ibid.*

25. Article 18.

26. Articles 6, 7, 18.

27. Articles 17, 20.

28. The earlier cases are treated in Edgar S. Furniss, Jr., "The Inter-American System and Present Caribbean Disputes," *International Organization*, IV (1950). These and more recent cases are treated in Pan American Union, *Applications of the Inter-American Treaty of Reciprocal Assistance, 1948–1956* (1957).

29. *Ibid.*, p. 19.

30. *Ibid.*, pp. 26–28, 48.

31. *Ibid.*, p. 109.

32. *Ibid.*, p. 111.

33. *Ibid.*, p. 115. Even the assumption that small powers cannot intervene in the affairs of great powers seems to have been challenged during these years. In 1954, a British investigation showed that definite assistance had been offered by the Guatemalan government to the Peoples United party of British Honduras, a party actively seeking separation from Britain. It showed

payment of $500 by the Guatemalan consul at Belize in connection with the costs of defense of party members on trial for sedition. It also showed that an extremely seditious broadcast was made from the Government Broadcasting Station in Guatemala City, based on materials supplied through the Peoples United party. Other less active support had also been offered by officials of the Guatemalan government: Reginald Sharpe, *British Honduras: Report of an Inquiry held by Sir Reginald Sharpe into Allegations of Contacts between the Peoples United party and Guatemala* (1954). During the 1958 congressional elections in the United States, an official of the Trujillo regime wrote letters to state party leaders in the United States urging the defeat of four congressmen who had been critical of Trujillo. See Charles O. Porter and Robert J. Alexander, *The Struggle for Democracy in Latin America* (New York, 1961), p. 155.

34. Inter-American Conference, Tenth, *Report of the Delegation of the United States of America* (1955), p. 157.
35. *Ibid.*, p. 9.
36. Resolutions XCIV and XCV, *ibid.*, pp. 158–159.
37. See Inter-American Conference, Tenth, *Actas y documentos*, II, especially pp. 262–265, 270–277, 286–290.
38. Refers to the Inter-American Treaty of Reciprocal Assistance (Rio Treaty), signed at Rio de Janeiro, Sept. 2, 1947. Article 6 provides that "If the inviolability or integrity of the territory or the sovereignty or political independence of any American State should be affected by an aggression which is not an armed attack or by an extra-continental or intra-continental conflict, or by any other fact or situation that might endanger the peace of America, the Organ of Consultation shall meet immediately in order to agree on the measures which must be taken in case of aggression to assist the victim of the aggression or, in any case, the measures which should be taken for common defense and for the maintenance of the peace and security of the Continent." Article 25 of the Charter of the O.A.S. incorporates this treaty by reference.
39. See, for example, the Panamanian, Bolivian, Uruguayan and Guatemalan amendments and resolutions in Inter-American Conference, Tenth, *Actas y documentos*, III, pp. 118, 278, 282–283, 292, 313.
40. Pan American Union, *Applications of the Inter-American Treaty of Reciprocal Assistance, 1948–1956*, p. 153.
41. *Ibid.*
42. O.A.S., Document C-a-155, *Acta de la Sesion Extraordinaria celebrada el 2 de julio de 1954* (1954), pp. 920–922.
43. *New York Times*, Feb. 20, 1959.
44. *Ibid.*
45. *La Prensa* (Buenos Aires), Aug. 15, 1959.
46. *La Prensa* (Lima), Aug. 15, 1959.
47. *Ibid.*, Aug. 12, Aug. 16; *La Prensa* (Buenos Aires), Aug. 16.
48. *Ibid.*, Aug. 15; *La Prensa* (Lima), Aug. 14.
49. *Ibid.*
50. U.S. Department of State, *Bulletin*, XLI (Sept. 7, 1959), pp. 343–344.
51. Pan American Union, 1960, p. 18.
52. U.S. Department of State, *Bulletin* (Sept. 5, 1960), pp. 355–359.

53. *Ibid.*, (Sept. 12, 1960), p. 408.
54. *New York Times*, Aug. 18, 1960.
55. *Ibid.*, Jan. 5, 1961.
56. U.S. Department of State, *Bulletin* (Aug. 29, 1960), p. 316; Council on Foreign Relations, *The United States in World Affairs, 1960* (New York, 1961), p. 318.
57. *New York Times*, Aug. 29, 1960.
58. *Ibid.*, April 21, 1961.
59. *The International Conferences of American States*, First Supplement, p. 160.
60. U.S. Department of State, *Bulletin*, XLI (Sept. 7, 1959), p. 343.
61. Ann Van Wynen Thomas and A. J. Thomas, Jr. *Non-Intervention: The Law and Its Import in the Americas* (Dallas, 1956), p. 389.
62. Uruguay, Ministerio de Relaciones Exteriores, *op. cit.*, p. 42.
63. *La Prensa* (Buenos Aires), Aug. 13, 1959.
64. *New York Times*, Jan. 31, 1960.
65. *Ibid.*, Feb. 8, 1960.
66. *Supra*, chapter 3.
67. *La Prensa* (Lima), Aug. 14, 1959.
68. *New York Times*, March 7, 1954.
69. Furniss, *op. cit.*, p. 597.
70. See his address given before the conference, "Freedom and the Dignity of Man," reprinted in *Vital Speeches*, Sept. 1, 1961, pp. 675–676. See also *New York Times*, Aug. 8–10, 1961.

Chapter Five

Diplomatic Asylum[1]

Historical development in Latin America

The practice of diplomatic asylum in Latin America is often traced to antecedents in ancient societies and to later practices in Europe, especially in Spain. But the development of the practice in Latin America seems to be less the result of a conscious application of any of these earlier patterns than the evolving of similar institutions as a product of human interaction confronted by similar circumstances at different times and places. It is true, of course, that the very circumstances that have been responsible for the origin and continuation of the practice of diplomatic asylum in Latin America are in part a product of Spanish culture which was transferred to the New World. It is, thus, best understood as an indiginous Latin American institution which has been the result of the peculiar political conditions and the cultural traditions of the area.

By diplomatic asylum we refer to the practice of granting protection within a premise claiming diplomatic immunity or inviolability (usually an embassy or legation) to an individual who is sought by the authorities of his own state. There is universal agreement that common criminals must not be afforded such protection. Diplomatic asylum is also used to refer to temporary protection granted to an individual who may be pursued by a mob or even by some indiscriminate official. But this creates few problems as long as the individual is surrendered to the proper authorities upon their demand. When the diplomatic representative refuses to surrender him to the proper authorities and asks that he be granted a guarantee of safe conduct out of the country, the real conflict arises. This amounts to removing the individual from the jurisdiction of his own state while he remains physically within it.

Throughout the colonial era in Latin America, the Church continued to grant asylum to individuals who were sought for one reason or another by the political-administrative representatives of the Spanish Crown. Numerous royal decrees were issued in order to limit and regulate this vexing practice, but only a very limited success was achieved.[2] Within limits, however, the practice could be safely tolerated. Both the Church and the temporal authorities in the colonies were under the Spanish Crown. Thus the granting of asylum in churches and other religious properties was far less of a threat to the Crown's authority than it would have been had the Church been an independent institution.

Shortly after the wars for independence in Latin America, the Church began to be shorn of many of its old privileges. In response to this, the clergy began to plunge into politics with greater enthusiasm than ever before, for they felt, quite correctly, that many of the political forces in the new republics were a real threat to their position. In these tumultuous years, asylum was often granted in churches and monasteries to enemies of the regime in power. With the clergy being a party to so many of the political struggles, a real threat was presented to any regime at odds with the Church. By the 1820's, state authorities began to enter churches and other religious properties in order to apprehend fugitives. By the 1830's, they had effectively demonstrated that such places were not always a safe refuge and, by the end of the decade, the practice of ecclesiastical asylum had all but disappeared.[3]

By this time, however, there were new and more effective places for granting asylum. The embassies and legations which were established as the new states gained independence were quite a different force to be reckoned with. The rule of inviolability of diplomatic premises had by this time become well established, and failure to observe it might well mean a rupture in diplomatic relations, a situation that precarious governments could hardly afford. Whenever the inviolability of an embassy or legation was threatened, and this has been true throughout the world, the diplomatic corps was quick to convene and act in unison.

Few details are available concerning the practice during the first

years of independence. By the middle of the nineteenth century, however, we find diplomatic correspondence referring to asylum as a common practice in many of the South (then common usage for "Latin")
American republics.[4] But if the practice was common, it was still far
from uncontested, and the United States was often involved in some
of the bitterest controversies. Although the latter has now managed
to extricate itself from this problem, it once presented some of the
most difficult dilemmas for the Department of State. The evolution
of United States policy from one of unhappy involvement to one of
relieved aloofness with regard to this important aspect of inter-American affairs will be outlined before we return to the Latin American
practice.

The United States escapes a dilemma

In one respect, at least, the policy of the United States toward the
question of diplomatic asylum has been entirely consistent. The Department of State has always denied that a right of asylum is sanctioned by general international law or by any regional rule of law
and has reminded its diplomatic representatives in Latin America of
this fact time after time.[5] But it soon became clear that this view of
the law could not be reconciled with the realities of political life in
Latin America. The United States Minister to Haiti, having been
harassed with this dilemma throughout his mission, complained to the
Department in 1899.

Not one of my predecessors has been able literally to carry out the instructions of the Department, and I am forced to add that it will be impossible for my successors to act differently from the course pursued by
their predecessors as long as the other legations receive and protect those
that come to them in such emergencies. . . . A refugee comes to us; asks
protection; we refuse to extend it to him; in return he refuses to leave the
premises. Are we to use force to compel him to leave?[6]

The fact is that the United States did allow its diplomatic representatives throughout Latin America to grant asylum and insisted that
this asylum be respeced. In order to make this action correspond to the
legal position it maintained, it was necessary to produce some rather
curious arguments. The main justification of a practice which we admitted had no legal foundation was that of "local toleration." In one
of the earlier cases (1851) in the records of American diplomatic
history, the Department advised its minister in Chile that

If there should be any precedent showing that the Chilean Government had previously acquiesced in such a proceeding on the part of a diplomatic representative of any foreign nation at Santiago, it could not justly complain of our course, unless formal notice should have previously been given that it would not in the future tolerate the exercise of the right.[7]

The policy was far from consistent, however, and there are numerous cases where the diplomatic representative has been reprimanded for having granted protection to a political refugee even in a country where the practice was commonplace. But usually the Department has stood behind him if it appeared that he had been left no choice. In some instances it has even supported him before the government to which he was accredited, only reprimanding him privately.[8]

Although, in the note quoted above, the idea of "local toleration" implies that the territorial state (the state in whose territory the embassy granting asylum is located) could terminate the practice if it so desired by merely declaring its intentions in advance, this has not in fact been the Department's interpretation. It has insisted that the state announcing such termination would have to make it effective for all other states represented there if the United States was to respect the announcement.[9] As early as 1867, the Minister to Peru admitted to that government, on just such an occasion, that it had every right to refuse to respect the practice of asylum. But, "notwithstanding this view," he said, "if the Government of Peru should feel disposed to concede greater privileges to others, I, as the representative of my Government, would expect to be entitled to the same privileges granted to them."[10]

Under these circumstances the United States has insisted that it was not simply a question to be decided by the territorial state alone, even if it should announce its intention to discontinue toleration of the practice *for all powers alike*. The powers represented in a particular country would also have to have a part in the decision—clearly a recognition of the fact that no such decision could be effective unless all powers agreed.

Our policy really amounted to saying that "we will *in fact* claim as a right what we do not *in theory* claim as a right." This curious legal status has been referred to by the Department of State as "a quasi rule of public law." Thus in 1879, it advised the Minister in Haiti that

If the so-called "right of asylum" (which this government has never been tenacious in claiming for its officers abroad) is to continue to exist as a quasi rule of public law, in communities where the conspirators of today may be the government of tomorrow, it should at least be so exercised as to afford no ground on the score of aiding and comforting rebellion.[11]

After about 1920 most of the Department's communications abandoned the argument of "local toleration" as a justification for its policy and emphasized, instead, purely humanitarian considerations. In the current Foreign Service Regulations, all reference to local practice or toleration has been deleted. They merely say that "Refuge may be afforded to uninvited fugitives whose lives are in imminent danger from mob violence but only for the period during which active danger continues."[12]

Although the regulations just quoted are currently in force, it has not been necessary to apply them in Latin America since the early 1930's. After 1931, public State Department records show no more cases of asylum granted in any of our diplomatic establishments in Latin America. Reports from two of our ministers, one in 1931 and one in 1932, are indicative of a new policy of extreme caution.

President resigned and is still in Moneda. Already he has requested asylum for his son-in-law and family and I have replied that I cannot admit them to the Embassy unless they are threatened with physical violence and then only temporarily.[13]

I have . . . been asked in several instances to shelter persons in my home or in the Chancery, I have consistently refused to grant such requests.[14]

This same attitude has been reflected in the position the United States has taken with regard to the three inter-American conventions on diplomatic asylum.* The first of these, the 1928 convention, was signed by the United States, but it had taken no part in the discussions and submitted a reservation stating that it did "not recognize or subscribe to, as a part of international law, the so-called doctrine of asylum."[15] It has declined to sign the two subsequent conventions and has not taken part in the discussions relating to either of them.[16]

These developments coincided with the period when the United States became increasingly sensitive to the charge of intervention in the domestic affairs of Latin America. Since the granting of diplomatic asylum easily lends itself to charges of this sort, and since the United States had never been anxious to continue the practice anyway, this was the perfect time to extricate itself from the whole vexing problem.

* For details see the following section.

The practice has thus become a *Latin* American problem rather than an *inter*-American problem, and it is to this more important aspect that we must now direct our attention.

Law or comity?

Latin American practice has been remarkably consistent in the sense that, when asylum has been granted within an embassy or legation, it has, with very few exceptions, been scrupulously respected. Not only has the refugee been allowed to remain unharmed within his place of asylum, but usually safe conduct out of the country has eventually been authorized, although long delays have not been uncommon.[17] The following are indicative of hundreds of cases which have been bitterly contested but amicably settled without either side clearly altering its legal position.

In 1858, three persons had taken refuge in the British and French legation (the two nations were occupying it jointly) in Venezuela. In the course of a long and bitter controversy, Venezuela threatened to give the ministers their passports, while the British and French warships threatened the port of La Guaira. After more than four months, a convention was signed which in fact provided for the safety of the refugees but also, as a face-saving measure, clearly implying the right of Venezuela to take such action against them as it might see fit. The provisions relating to one of the refugees who, according to the British and French, had been taken from the legation, are illustrative. The man was to be returned to the British and French legation and then "placed at the disposition of the Venezuelan government as soon as it may demand it, unless before the solicitation is made he may be pardoned by the executive power of the Chief of State."[18]

Nearly a century later, in 1946, Bolivia suffered one of the more bitter and violent revolutions which have so often plagued that country. A large number of the officials and supporters of the deposed Villarroel regime took refuge in several of the embassies and legations in La Paz. For nearly five months, many of the refugees were demanded for "crimes of Nazism," crimes against humanity and various common crimes. Yet, after all this, they were eventually allowed to leave the country.[19]

About two years later Haya de la Torre, the leader of the Peruvian Apra party, was forced to take refuge in the Colombian embassy in Lima. The Peruvians demanded him for "terrorism" and other crimes.

He remained there during more than four years of diplomatic controversy, which finally brought the case before the International Court of Justice. Following two inconclusive decisions by the Court, the two countries reached an agreement which permitted Haya to leave the country, although each party preserved its legal position.[20]

But when we move from the bare fact of practice to the attitudes concerning the legal foundations for the practice, and thus the extent of legal right or obligation involved, it is quite a different matter. The jurist generally insists that mere practice is not sufficient to create a customary rule of law. Practice must be accompanied by the conviction that it was legally obligatory—*opinio juris sive necessitatus*.[21] Here the Latin American record can only be described as inconsistent. In most instances the legal foundations of the institution are not even discussed or at best are referred to only in the most ambiguous terms. When the legal foundations are discussed, governments have at times insisted and at other times denied that the practice has any basis in law. They have insisted that there is a "right of asylum" when one of their own embassies has granted protection to a political refugee, only to take the opposite position a few years later when some foreign embassy does the same thing.[22]

Even when the granting of asylum gives rise to no controversy and the refugee is permitted to leave the country, it is difficult to assess the exact legal significance. In some cases the government of the territorial state is happy to find a means of getting the individual out of the country; to shield him from momentary public indignation; or to offer a face-saving explanation if it is not anxious to carry out the "just punishment" it has publicly promised for members of a deposed regime. The territorial state, in granting a safe-conduct out of the country, may also welcome it as a form of "expulsion" for persons whom it considers undesirable or dangerous to have around—indeed it has at times used the term "expulsion" instead of "safe-conduct."

Often there are no charges against an individual, and only his own suspicions have driven him to seek refuge. Under these circumstances the territorial state usually has no objection to guaranteeing him safe-conduct out of the country. Finally, the refugee sometimes leaves the embassy after a few hours, and often the territorial state may not even have been aware of his presence there.[23]

A combination of these circumstances was described by the United States *chargé d'affaires* in Cuba in 1932. He had inquired about an opposition leader, a Dr. de la Cruz, who was rumored to have sought refuge in the United States embassy in Havana. He told the Department of State that the Cuban Secretary of Foreign Affairs had "replied that he understood that de la Cruz was in the Uruguayan Legation and that if this were true, the Cuban Government would raise no objection. He regarded such asylum as entirely justifiable in the circumstances, since it might protect the refugee from acts which the Cuban Government would be the first to condemn. Furthermore, de la Cruz was not a fugitive from justice."[24]

Even when states have clearly claimed or admitted a "right of asylum," they have not committed themselves to anything very concrete. There is universal agreement that this really means "right of asylum for political refugees"—no one has ever claimed or admitted that this applied to common criminals. But the line between a political offense and a common crime is nearly always a fine one indeed. It is easy to declare a refugee a "common criminal" ineligible for asylum, while insisting that the true principle of a right of asylum for political offenses is still respected. Thus in a great many of these controversies, governments are able to avoid taking any position on whether a right of asylum exists in American international law. They will insist that it is unnecessary to consider this since the case at hand involves a common criminal ineligible for asylum in any event.

The Convention on Asylum, signed at Havana in 1928, attempted to clarify the legal status of the institution. But the document only reflects the general reluctance to accept a firm commitment. The second article of this ambiguous convention is the most important. It provides that "Asylum granted to political offenders in legations, warships, military camps or military aircraft, shall be respected to the extent in which allowed, as a right or through humanitarian toleration, by the usages, the conventions or the laws of the country in which granted."[25] The difficult task of defining a "political offender" is understandably not undertaken in the treaty. The additional qualification that "asylum may not be granted except for urgent cases and for the period of time strictly indispensable for the person who is sought to ensure in some other way his safety" only provides new sources of disagreement in the absence of any definition of an "urgent case."[26]

The applications of this treaty, now in force among fifteen Latin American states, show how nebulous is the commitment to respect "asylum granted to political offenders." The test came with the political upheavals that moved across Latin America in the early 1930's. Conflicts between states which had ratified the treaty now dealt with the qualification of the offense rather than with the principle of a right of asylum. If the territorial state had any objections to allowing refugees to leave the country, it would insist that they were common criminals and thus, under the 1928 treaty, could not legally be given asylum.

If Latin American practice had shown some fairly consistent pattern in defining a "political offender" as distinguished from a "common criminal," it would have facilitated the application of the convention. But the diplomatic exchanges relating to asylum controversies offer little assistance indeed. They do show that the diplomatic representative has granted asylum when he suspected that the person seeking it was pursued for political reasons, but if the representative had any clear criteria for determining whether or not this was really the case, these criteria have not been revealed in the exchanges that followed. In short, it has been a highly subjective and intuitive process on the part of the diplomatic representative.[27]

Thus, in actual practice, the 1928 convention did not really settle very much. In an effort to narrow the area of conflict, a Convention on Political Asylum was proposed at the Seventh International Conference of American States in 1933. The subcommittee that prepared the draft for this convention summarized accurately and briefly the failure of the previous agreement. "Since the signing of the Havana Convention of 1928," it observed, "differences of interpretation have arisen, causing painful controversies which have menaced cordiality. . . . The one receiving asylum has been indefinitely held in the legation in an embarrassing situation, converting it into a veritable prison."[28]

The new convention again wisely avoided the futile task of trying to define a "political offender." Instead, it provided that "the judgment of political delinquency concerns the State which offers asylum."[29] Although the language of this official translation is somewhat obscure, there never seems to have been any doubt that it authorized the state granting asylum to decide whether the refugee was being sought for political reasons. But does this mean that the granting state may decide the question temporarily or definitively? A few minor controversies arose rather soon after the convention was signed, but the real test came in the wake of the political disturbances following World War II.

In the Dominican Republic, during 1945, a number of persons sought refuge from the vindictiveness of the Trujillo regime. To the diplomatic representatives who had granted asylum in their premises, the Dominican government argued that the 1933 treaty allowed only a *provisional* qualification of the offense "as a point of departure for study of the case by the interested governments." "Anything else," it argued, "would openly abandon the most elementary attributes of national sovereignty."[30]

Three years later, when Haya de la Torre was granted asylum in the Colombian embassy in Lima, Peru, the Peruvian government advanced the same argument (even though it had not ratified this convention and was not bound by it). It also raised the arguments that the 1928 convention had authorized the granting of asylum only for urgent cases and that neither the 1933 convention nor any other indicated which party had a right to qualify these circumstances.[31]

Still another question of interpretation was raised when the Guatemalan embassy in Nicaragua granted asylum to a military officer who had been engaged in certain political activities for which he was sought by the Nicaraguan government. The latter argued that the officer had left his post, that he was a military deserter, and that the right of unilateral qualification of the nature of the offense would thus not apply. The Guatemalan government asserted that "the fact of abandoning his post does not necessarily imply manifest intentions of abandonment of duty. . . . It is simply the consequence of other acts of a political character which compelled him to take refuge, although to do so he would have to abandon the performance of his charge."[32]

In the increasing bitterness of actual and incipient social revolutions, it should not be surprising to discover that interpretations were found to meet the needs of governments threatened by them. At the same time, some governments were convinced that it was now more important than ever to preserve an institution which offered at least some humanitarian recourse in these bitter struggles.

At the Tenth Inter-American Conference in 1954, another effort was made to clarify rights and duties concerning the granting of asylum—especially those that were still left uncertain under the 1933 convention. In the Convention on Diplomatic Asylum, signed at the Tenth Conference, the granting state is again authorized to qualify the nature of the offense. But under this convention the granting state may also request that the refugee "be allowed to depart for foreign territory, and the territorial state is under obligation to grant immediately, except in case of *force majeure*, the necessary guarantees . . . as well as the corresponding safe conduct."[33]

This statement clearly removes all doubt concerning "temporary" or "definitive" qualification of the offense, at least until after the refugee has left the country. Then the only recourse open to the territorial state is to request extradition through normal channels. If the territorial state informs the diplomatic representative of its intention to request extradition, the refugee must be kept within the territory of the state granting asylum until such a request is received—but the period of time must not exceed thirty days. Finally, asylum is to be granted only in urgent cases, but the granting state is permitted to determine the degree of urgency.[34]

Only seven Latin American states have ratified this convention,[35] probably a reflection of the explicitness of the rights and obligations set forth in it. In view of the small number of states that had ratified, a number of proposals that would make it more acceptable to a larger number of states were submitted for consideration by the Inter-American Juridical Committee. Two of the proposals called for a committee of investigation to qualify the nature of the offense when there might be disagreement between the two parties. Another would set up a simple procedure whereby the territorial state, after the safe-conduct had been granted to the refugee, might request the supreme court of the state granting asylum to review the decision of the diplomatic agent or of the foreign ministry of that country.[36]

The Juridical Committee did not feel that the proposals for committees of investigation with the authority to qualify the nature of the offense would offer any advantages over the present treaty provisions. It felt that these proposals would amount to a system of arbitration which, under the circumstances, would have disadvantages. Under the present system, the Committee observed, "there is neither victor nor vanquished, as there is in the case of arbitration, where one of the parties is defeated when its theses are found to be without basis. This undoubtedly affects the prestige of the state for which the award is unfavorable, and may bring about unexpected reactions in the public opinion of that state."[37]

The proposal that would authorize the territorial state to request the supreme court of the state granting asylum to review the qualification of the offense was also questioned by the Committee, since it noted that this would be complicated by constitutional provisions in some of the states. It recommended, instead, that an attempt be made to improve the provisions under which the territorial state could request extradition after the refugee had left the country. Such a provision, it felt, would accomplish the same thing since the supreme court in each of the countries would be in a position to review these cases, a procedure which the Committee felt would be beneficial. It would provide the opportunity whereby a case could be reviewed by persons of outstanding moral and professional character after the immediate tensions are lessened and after passions have lost much of their violence. In order to improve these provisions of the 1954 convention, it recommended that the refugee be required to remain in the country granting him asylum (to which he would have been granted safe conduct) "for a period of 60 days with a view to the possible presentation of a request for extradition." Thus the territorial state would not have to indicate in advance of the safe-conduct whether or not it intended to request extradition.[38]

No action has yet been taken on these proposals, but they will undoubtedly come up for consideration at the next inter-American conference, which is now overdue.

Social needs and the survival of a unique institution

Both practice and treaties show that Latin American states have been reluctant to admit *without qualification* that they will be legally bound to respect a right of asylum for political offenders and that the refugee must be permitted to leave the country at the request of the state granting him asylum. Only the 1954 Convention on Diplomatic Asylum includes such provisions in nearly absolute terms, and this convention has received by far the smallest number of ratifications— only seven to date. We have already noted that two previous conventions were signed, apparently with this purpose in mind, but that interpretations which deprived them of most of their meaning were soon found.

Whether or not this practice now responds to a generally accepted rule of law is less important than the fact that it is almost universally respected throughout Latin America. It is an institution which has developed in response to the social needs of these societies and reflects the culture and traditions of the area. The very fact that it is one of the few "rules" which have been able to survive the impact of social revolution and cold war is proof of its viability. Even though, in 1954, the Dominican Republic denounced the conventions of 1928 and 1933, it has in fact continued to respect the practice and has granted safe-conduct out of the country for the refugees.[39] The bitterness and violence of the Cuban social revolution have also stopped short of trying to destroy this institution. There are arguments and delays, to be sure, but with very few exceptions the refugee is eventually permitted to leave the country in safety.[40]

Why, then, the reluctance to make an unqualified and unambiguous commitment? First of all, it must be noted that this is an institution very susceptible to abuse and, if abused, it is an open invitation to plotting and insurrection against a government. It creates especially delicate problems because it is closely linked with the most vital of all rules in international society—the immunity of diplomatic officers and the inviolability of embassies and legations. These rules can be violated only at the risk of interrupting vital international intercourse. The present somewhat nebulous status of the institution at least allows the territorial state some measure of regulation and control. It is *not* likely that the states which have refused to commit themselves more explicitly on this are contemplating at some future date the possibility of forcing the surrender of a refugee from a diplomatic establishment. Rather, they are reserving for future use the weapons of indefinite delay in granting safe-conduct and of other inconveniences which can be inflicted upon the embassy or legation that abuses the privilege. These weapons provide some measure of protection against too extravagant an application of the practice. The more precise the commitment to respect the practice, the more difficult it becomes to apply measures of delay and inconvenience.

Many who would prefer a better-defined inter-American legal order have argued that the provisions of the 1954 Convention on Diplomatic Asylum are so well established in practice that they may be regarded as customary rules of law. These provisions were essentially what the International Court of Justice was asked to declare as law in the *Colombian-Peruvian Asylum Case* of 1950 involving Haya de la Torre. Since both states had ratified the 1928 convention, the principle of a right of asylum for *political* offenders was not an issue. But Peru had not ratified the 1933 convention which provided for unilateral qualification of the offense by the state granting asylum. Colombia argued that the 1933 convention was now only declaratory of a customary rule of law, in other words, that a customary rule of law had evolved allowing the state granting asylum to qualify the nature of the offense.[41]

The Court held that the evidence presented did not show the existence of any such customary rule. For reasons that need not be discussed here, the Court also ruled that asylum had been *prolonged* for reasons not recognized by the 1928 convention, yet it ruled that Colombia was not required to surrender the refugee and Peru was not required to grant him safe-conduct out of the country.[42]

The decision was greeted with considerable dismay, especially among a number of Latin American jurists. But would it have made the practice into a more effective institution had the Court decided that unilateral qualification of the offense by the state granting asylum was sanctioned by *law?* Or is it possible that such a ruling would have made the practice less viable? There is at least some reason to consider the second a more probable development.

Clearly the case was left as unsettled as it had been before the endless learned arguments and counterarguments had been offered to the Court. But this is precisely the wisdom of the decision. The Court refused to apply rules for which it could not find definitive evidence and left the matter to be settled the way thousands of asylum cases have been settled in the past. An amicable solution is eventually worked out which may or may not be the result of legal considerations, but the refugee is, almost without exception, permitted to leave the country. This is precisely what happened with Haya de la Torre.

Had the Court insisted on putting this practice into a legal mold, it is by no means clear that it would have had a beneficial effect on the institution of asylum. How many states would then have announced that they would not in the future tolerate the practice (as the Dominican Republic did in 1954)? Would the diplomatic representative continue to use the same caution when the law was more clearly on his side?

All of this clearly points to the wisdom of Charles de Visscher's admonition that he who would understand the international legal order must not see "in the process by which norms are formed only the special procedure that constitutes the last phase and marks its full achievement."[43] The normative function of well-established practices which are not necessarily regarded as "law" should not be underestimated. Here is a practice which has responded to the unstable and often violent political climate of Latin America for more than a century. We have already suggested that the rather ambiguous nature of the obligations which states recognize with regard to this practice has provided a measure of flexibility and control. The increased bitterness of social revolutions in many parts of Latin America will certainly place new strains on the practice at the very time when the humanitarian purpose it has served becomes more important than ever before.

The fact that the United States has been able to extricate itself from the practice has removed at least one complicating element. Should the United States again become involved, the problem would become infinitely more complex.[44] The granting of asylum to political offenders can easily be a means of intervention in the domestic politics of another state. It is probably more than mere coincidence that the United States ended the practice in the very years when complaints against Yankee intervention were the bitterest and when the new non-intervention policy was emerging.

Given the continued "disengagement" of the United States, the flexible nature of the institution of diplomatic asylum holds out the hope that it will be able to survive contemporary upheavals. That it is a product of Latin American traditions, responding to the peculiar needs of these societies, explains its survival when so many of the traditional rules of international law are challenged or ignored.

FOOTNOTES

1. Chapter Five is based primarily on a Ph.D. dissertation by the author: *The Legal Status of the Institution of Diplomatic Asylum in Latin America as Determined by Treaties and Practice* (Ann Arbor, Mich., University Microfilm, 1958).
2. Adolfo Molino Orantes, "Aspectos históricos de asilo en Guatemala," *Revista de la asociación guatemalteca de derecho internacional* (Guatemala, Jan. 1954), pp. 106–119; Domingo Cavalario, *Instituciones de derecho canónico* (Valencia, 1846); Alejandro Maure, *Bosquejo histórico de las revoluciones de Centro America* (Paris, 1913); Mario del Valle Muñoz, *El derecho de asilo eclesiástico en el reino de Chile* (Santiago, 1952?).
3. See especially Molino Orantes, *op. cit.*, and del Valle Muñoz, *op. cit.*
4. See cases discussed in Ronning, *op. cit.*, especially chapters 2 and 6.
5. *Ibid.*, chapter 6.
6. *Foreign Relations of the U.S.*, 1899, p. 394.
7. J. B. Moore, *Digest*, II, pp. 787–788.
8. Ronning, *op. cit.*, pp. 74 ff.
9. *Ibid.*, pp. 162 ff.
10. *Foreign Relations of the U.S.*, 1867, II, pp. 738–739.
11. *Foreign Relations of the U.S.*, 1879, p. 582.
12. 1 *FSM* I 225.2, issued under TL: A-66, Feb. 12, 1952, revalidated March 30, 1956.
13. G. H. Hackworth, *Digest*, I, p. 905.
14. *Foreign Relations of the U.S.*, 1932, V, p. 559. This course was approved by the Department, *ibid.*, p. 560.
15. International Conference of American States, Sixth, *Report of the Delegates of the United States* (Washington, D.C., 1928), p. 19.
16. Ronning, *op. cit.*, pp. 193–194.
17. See cases discussed in detail, *ibid.*, chapters 5, 6 and 9.
18. Convention signed at La Guaira, Aug. 27, 1858, reprinted in Simón Planas-

Suarez, *El asilo diplomático* (Buenos Aires, 1953), pp. 482–483. For further details on the case see Ronning, *op. cit.*, pp. 41–42, 246 ff.

19. *Ibid.*, p. 141.
20. *New York Times*, March 24, 1954.
21. See L. F. Oppenheim, *International Law: A Treatise* (8th ed. by H. Lauterpacht, London, 1955), vol. I, pp. 25–27.
22. Cases are treated in detail in Ronning, *op. cit.*, chapter 5.
23. *Ibid.*, chapter 3.
24. *Foreign Relations of the U.S.*, 1932, V, p. 558.
25. International Conference of American States, Sixth, *Final Act* (Havana, 1928), p. 166.
26. *Ibid.*
27. See cases discussed in Ronning, *op. cit.*, chapter 9.
28. M. O. Hudson, *International Legislation*, VI, p. 610.
29. *Ibid.*
30. Manuel Arturo Peña Batlle, *"Una sentencia de la Corte Internacional de Justicia,"* *El Caribe* (Ciudad Trujillo), April 8, 1951. Peña Batlle was then Secretary of Foreign Relations.
31. See exchange of notes reproduced in Peru, Ministerio de Relaciones Exteriores, *Proceso sobre asilo entre el Peru y Colombia ante la Corte Internacional de Justicia: documentación pertinente al desarrollo del juicio sentencia del 20 de noviembre de 1950* (Lima, 1950), especially pp. 5 ff.
32. *Diario de Centro America*, May 24, 1954.
33. Pan American Union, *Convention on Diplomatic Asylum Signed at the Tenth Inter-American Conference, Caracas, March 28, 1954*, Law and Treaty Series (Washington, 1954).
34. *Ibid.*
35. Pan American Union, *Tratados y convenciones inter-americanos*, Serie sobre tratados (Washington, D.C., 1957), p. 48.
36. Inter-American Juridical Committee, *New Articles on Diplomatic Asylum* (Washington, D.C., 1960), pp. 1–5.
37. *Ibid.*, pp. 10–11.
38. *Ibid.*, pp. 12–14.
39. Dominican Republic, *Gaceta oficial* (Ciudad Trujillo, Sept. 27, 1954), pp. 9–11.
40. On Sept. 1, 1961, the Venezuelan Consul General in Havana reported that the Cuban government had granted safe-conduct passes to 800 persons who had been granted asylum in various embassies and legations there. Some of the 220 refugees in the Venezuelan embassy had already arrived in Venezuela. See *New York Times*, Sept. 2, 1961.
41. See Peru, Ministerio de Relaciones Exteriores, *Proceso sobre Asilo . . .*, pp. 349 ff.
42. *Colombian-Peruvian Asylum Case, Judgment of November 20th, 1950: I.C.J. Reports 1950*; and *Haya de la Torre Case, Judgment of June 13th, 1951: I.C.J. Reports, 1951*.
43. Charles de Visscher, *op. cit.*, p. xii.
44. The United States became involved in a case when in November 1956 Cardinal Mindszenty took asylum in the United States legation in Hungary. On November 13, 1956, *The New York Times* reported that the White House had confirmed the receipt of a letter from Cardinal Mindszenty, reported to

have been carried from Hungary by a correspondent of the North American Newspaper Alliance. The letter said in part: "as a shipwreck of Hungarian liberty I have been taken aboard by your generosity in a refuge of my own country as a guest of your legation. Your hospitality surely saved me from immediate death."

Chapter Six

Territorial Waters and Beyond

The rise and decline of the "three-mile rule"

All states bordering on an ocean claim a maritime belt or zone which, in contrast to the open sea, is under the jurisdiction of the littoral state. This belt is usually referred to as "territorial sea" or "territorial waters." States generally agree that the nature of their jurisdiction over this area "amounts to sovereignty" and "that the maritime belt is a part of the territory of the littoral state,"[1] subject only to the right of "innocent passage." A more limited jurisdiction is also often exercised over a belt of water beyond, but bordering upon, the territorial sea. This area is generally referred to as a "contiguous zone."

But there has been far less agreement concerning the *extent* of these zones or belts. Differing claims over large expanses of ocean are as old as the state system in international relations. Although only a few of the more powerful maritime states have been able to claim entire seas, a great many states have made extensive claims to jurisdiction over waters touching upon their shores—up to one hundred miles in a number of cases. After the eighteenth century, however, a limit of one marine league came to be recognized by most states as the proper breadth of the territorial sea. It was, of course, no mere coincidence that this practice gained wide application along with the emergence of the balance of power system, and that it reflected the interests of its members.

The United States, shortly after achieving its independence, announced that it would limit its jurisdiction to three miles beyond its shore, although Secretary of State Jefferson noted that great differences of opinion existed on this point and that the United States might in the future extend its jurisdiction beyond three miles, "after respectful and friendly communication."[2] With some exceptions, however, the three-mile rule has remained the standard for United States policy. Between 1886 and 1890 the United States attempted to regulate seal fishing in the Bering Sea as far as one hundred Italian miles from the lands purchased from Russia in 1867. But under threat of forceful resistance from Britain, the United States agreed to submit the claim to arbitration and accepted the commission's ruling that it had no right to exercise this jurisdiction outside the three-mile limit.[3]

Another exception to this limit has been made for sanitary regulation and customs control. Since 1799, the United States has claimed a limited jurisdiction up to twelve miles for such purposes. This was extended by the Anti-Smuggling Act of 1935 which authorized the President to declare a limited customs enforcement area up to a total distance of sixty-two miles from the coast.[4] Virtually all states now claim the right to exercise a similar limited jurisdiction beyond the three-mile zone. But again there is little agreement on the exact distance or the extent of jurisdiction within the area. It may be regarded as established practice, however, that a state may push its law enforcement activity at least twelve miles seaward.

All these practices of course developed out of a long series of claims, protests and coercive measures undertaken by those who were in a position to do so. The literature of international law is full of protests against various extensions of jurisdiction, even when the protesting state claimed for itself the very right against which it protested. But, although agreement has been neither universal nor precise, there has existed within the broad limits described what might be called a "consensus." This position, shared generally by all the great maritime powers of the world, has reflected an interest in opening the seas to free navigation for the commercial and fishing interests of the senior members of the community. Their security has also required a maximum freedom for naval forces in time of war as well as in time of peace.

The interests of Latin American states in the nineteenth and early twentieth century presented few obstacles to the application of the doctrine of open seas. The dominant agricultural and commercial interests desired a maximum of free trade, and security depended on Britain or the United States. For about a century, the question of jurisdiction over territorial waters and contiguous zones caused little trouble in inter-American relations.[5]

Changes in the international power structure no less than changes in the economic, political and social structure of Latin American states have now challenged the "old consensus" which supported the freedom of the seas. Recent technological developments altering the relationship between national societies and the sea around them have also entered the picture. The impact of these forces on the positions that American states have taken with regard to adjacent seas will be the theme of our account of the breakup of an old "consensus" and the efforts to arrive at a new one.

The narrowing of the high seas

The first inter-American action relating to the question of jurisdiction over coastal waters reflected the early hopes of the United States to isolate the Western Hemisphere from the violence of World War II. At the meeting of foreign ministers in Panama, in September and October of 1939, the United States pressed for approval of various resolutions and declarations with this purpose in mind.[6] The Declaration of Panama proclaimed the "inherent right" of the American Republics "to have those waters adjacent to the American continent, which they regard of primary concern and direct utility in their relations, free from commission of any hostile act by any non-American belligerent nation." The declaration went on to define a maritime belt, exceeding three hundred miles in breadth at some points, from the Atlantic boundary of the United States and Canada around the Western Hemisphere to the Pacific boundary of the same. It was agreed that, within this "security zone," the American republics would endeavor "to secure compliance" by the belligerents "with the provisions of this Declaration."[7]

Early replies to this declaration by the three belligerents—England, France and Germany—stated that the principle formulated would amount to a change in accepted practice, requiring the consent of the states affected.[8] This position was also taken by the legal advisor to the Peruvian Ministry of Foreign Affairs, in a report which he submitted shortly after the declaration had been invoked.

In the light of the principles considered in this study, the continental security zone proclaimed at the Panama Conference of 1939 . . . has no juridical base. Furthermore, it is necessary to keep in mind that the belligerent states in the European War have expressed unequivocally that they do not accept the unilateral demarkation of such a neutrality zone; even though in good will they have not brought the war into the vicinity of the American continent, these manifestations are only diplomatic courtesy which does not modify their rights under international law.[9]

Secretary of State Cordell Hull was equally skeptical, but the matter of legality was not allowed to stand in the way. He later recorded that he had questioned the declarations on the grounds that "it had no precedent in International law and could be objected to by the belligerents." But, since the President had "wholeheartedly embraced it," he was "willing to go along with him and see how it would work out."[10] He found, however, that it was no easy job to enlist the support of all the Latin American states. Under the leadership of Argentina, a number of South American states with long exposed coastlines feared that this was only asking for trouble with the Axis powers and questioned the ability of the United States to offer them the necessary protection should they be threatened.[11]

The next steps in the extension of jurisdiction came on the heels of World War II. On September 28, 1945, the President of the United States issued two important proclamations concerning national exploitation of the resources of the continental shelf and national regulation of contiguous fisheries. The first of these[12] began by asserting that efforts to discover and make available new sources of petroleum and other minerals should be encouraged, that many such resources underlie parts of the continental shelf, that jurisdiction over these resources is required for purposes of conservation and prudent utilization, and "that the exercise of jurisdiction over natural resources of the subsoil and sea bed of the continental shelf by the contiguous nation is reasonable and just." It was considered reasonable and just, according to the proclamation, since effective exploitation and conservation would depend on "cooperation and protection from the shore, since the continental shelf may be regarded as an extension of the land mass of the coastal nation and thus naturally appurtenant to it," and "since these resources frequently form a seaward extension of a pool or deposit lying within the territory." Thus the proclamation went on to say that "the Government of the United States regards the natural resources and subsoil of the continental shelf beneath the high seas but contiguous to the coast of the United States as appertaining to the United States, subject to its jurisdiction and control." Finally, it declared that "the character as high seas of the waters above the continental shelf and the right to their free and unimpeded navigation are in no way thus affected."

The second proclamation[13] was introduced with a reference to "the inadequacy of present arrangements for the protection and perpetuation of the fishery resources, contiguous to" the coasts of the United States and the "special importance of such fishery resources to coastal communities as a source of livelihood and to the nation as a food and industrial resource." Thus the government of the United States would regard it "as proper to establish conservation zones in those areas of the high seas contiguous to the coasts of the United States wherein fishing activities have been or in the future may be developed and maintained by its nationals alone." Where there had been joint development of such resources by nationals of the United States or where such development might occur in the future, "explicitly bounded conservation zones may be established under agreements between the United States and such other states." The right of other states to establish similar zones off their coasts "in accordance with the above principles" was conceded. Finally, "the character as high seas of the areas in which such conservation zones are established and rights to free and unimpeded navigation" were not to be affected.

Latin American decrees and constitutional amendments soon followed the United States proclamations. For the sake of convenience, the Latin American measures may be discussed in three broad categories.[14]

One category was of essentially the same limited nature as the United States proclamation on the continental shelf. These decrees, issued by Brazil, the Dominican Republic, Guatemala, Nicaragua and Venezuela, claimed jurisdiction over the continental shelf but left the superjacent waters unaffected.

More ambitious declarations were issued by Argentina, Honduras and Mexico. Argentina, by presidential decree of October 11, 1946, claimed jurisdiction not only over the continental shelf but over the waters covering it as well. The decree declared "the Argentine Epicontinental Sea [defined as "waters covering the submarine platform"] and the Continental shelf subject to the sovereign power of the nation." With a continental shelf extending at some points to one thousand kilometers from the shore, this provision would place hundreds of miles of high seas under Argentine jurisdiction. A Honduran constitutional amendment of 1950 contained a similar pronouncement. Somewhat more modest were the Mexican pronouncements which, by a proclamation of 1954, claimed "each and all of the natural resources of the continental shelf." In the waters above the continental shelf, Mexico claimed the paramount right to control fishing zones but not exclusive fishing rights.

Some of the more extensive claims, made by Chile, Costa Rica, Ecuador, El Salvador and Peru, have reversed the method of using the continental shelf as a measure of the seaward distance to which jurisdiction over coastal waters is claimed. Usually lacking an extensive continental shelf, they have declared "sole sovereignty and jurisdiction" over an expanse of adjacent sea up to two hundred miles and then have proclaimed a similar status for the sea bed and subsoil beneath it.[15]

In 1956, the representatives of Chile, Costa Rica, Peru and Ecuador modified their claims by explaining to the United Nations General Assembly that their respective governments had intended only to proclaim fishing and conservation authority and had not intended to extend their territorial waters to two hundred miles.[16] The character of these waters as high seas, they said, would not be affected—a somewhat ambiguous statement since they would clearly be subject to the restrictions necessary to conserve and exploit fisheries, seabed and subsoil resources.

Article 7 of the Constitution of El Salvador seems to claim rights much like the original claims of Chile, Costa Rica, Peru and Ecuador, but in language open to a variety of interpretations. It provides that "the territory of the Republic . . . includes the adjacent sea within a distance of two hundred marine miles . . . and it embraces the air space above, the subsoil and the corresponding shelf." Again, it stated that this does not affect "freedom of navigation in accordance with principles accepted by international law."[17]

The precise meaning of the claims made in many of these Latin American proclamations and constitutional provisions remains to be clarified. Positions are already in the process of being modified and will undoubtedly see further modification in the future. Although many of the original statements seemed to imply that areas of ocean up to two hundred miles would be reduced to the same status as waters within the old three-mile limit, other statements seem to contradict this. A number of states, while making these extensive but somewhat vague claims, continue to claim a much narrower belt as their "territorial sea." A listing prepared for the opening of the Geneva Conference on the Law of the Sea (1958) gave the following as the breadth of "territorial sea" claimed by Latin American states:

Argentina, Brazil, Cuba and the Dominican Republic, three miles; Colombia and Uruguay, six miles; Mexico, nine miles; Guatemala, Panama and Venezuela, twelve miles; Chile, fifty kilometers; El Salvador, two hundred miles.[18]

Inter-American and United Nations efforts

At its first meeting, in 1950, the Inter-American Council of Jurists charged its permanent committee, the Inter-American Juridical Committee, with the task of studying the "regime of the territorial sea and related questions." A majority of the committee members (Argentina, Chile, Mexico and Peru) represented states claiming a generous extension of jurisdiction over territorial seas. They took advantage of the opportunity to prepare a draft convention, accommodating the most extensive claims made by Latin American states, over strong minority objections (Brazil, Colombia and the United States).[19]

By the draft convention, the signatory states recognized that "present international law" granted to a littoral nation "exclusive sovereignty over the soil, subsoil, and waters on its continental shelf, and the airspace and stratosphere above it." The states with a very narrow continental shelf also received "the right of each of them to establish an area of protection, control and economic exploitation, to a distance of two hundred nautical miles from the low water mark along its coasts."[20]

The statement of reasons accompanying the draft convention noted that "very few of the important considerations upon which it is founded are conclusive," but stressed that a majority of American states have tacitly or expressly repudiated the three-mile rule. Noting that there were divergent American claims, it saw a "new rule of international law, too respectable and well founded to be repudiated, but at the same time imperfect." Thus the draft represented a "sincere desire to make the provisions consistent with the theoretical or rational evolution of international law relative to the *de facto* situation" in which the American states find themselves. It was admitted that international law cannot be established by a few states alone, but emphasized that "it is also true that a specific rule can be adopted by a few states to be in force between them and many times this procedure has been the origin of a universal rule."

The dissenting statement, signed by the delegates from Brazil, Colombia and the United States, objected to the fact that the committee had gone beyond its duties. In their opinion, the committee should have prepared a report on the assigned study and not a draft convention. They also objected to the arbitrary two-hundred-mile limit, the reference to "exclusive sovereignty over the soil, subsoil and waters" of the continental shelf, and to the failure to define the continental shelf while declaring territorial sovereignty over it.[21] Later, the Brazilian government offered the additional objection that since this problem was worldwide, there was no reason for trying to provide a regional solution. For such a solution, it said, could have no practical value unless accepted by the majority of the other nations.[22]

When the Inter-American Council of Jurists* considered the draft convention at their second meeting in 1953, there was, quite understandably, little agreement. In its *Final Act*, the best that the council could do was declare that "it is an obvious fact that development of technical methods for exploring and exploiting the riches of these zones has had as a consequence the recognition by international law of the right of such states to protect, conserve and promote these riches, as well as to insure for themselves the use and benefit thereof."[23] The United States objected to this statement on the grounds that it approved as an existing right a matter that has not been clearly settled in international law.[24] The report on territorial waters and related questions was sent back to the committee for further study.

In the meantime Chile, Ecuador and Peru held a meeting in Santiago, in an effort to consolidate their positions and set up machinery for joint action. In a "Declaration on the Maritime Zone," dated August 17, 1952, the three governments stated essentially their original positions as outlined in the previous section. In addition, they provided for the establishment of a Permanent Commission for the Exploitation and Conservation of the Maritime Resources of the South Pacific. Its purpose was to unify fishing and whaling regulations and to promote and coordinate conservation and scientific investigation.[25]

In 1954, the Tenth Inter-American Conference recommended that the Council of the O.A.S. convene a specialized conference to study the economic and juridical aspects of the regimen of the continental shelf, the waters of the sea and its natural resources. Convened at Cuidad Trujillo the following year, this conference was able to agree that the seabed and subsoil of the continental shelf, adjacent to the coastal state to a depth of two hundred meters or, beyond that limit, to where the depth allows exploitation of natural resources, "apper-

* All the American states are represented on the Council.

tain exclusively to that state and are subject to its jurisdiction and control."[26] Beyond this, the conference could only state that "agreement does not exist among the states here represented with respect to the juridical regime of the waters which cover the said submarine areas, nor with respect to the problem of whether certain living resources belong to the sea bed or to the superjacent waters."[27]

The third meeting of the Inter-American Council of Jurists (1956) provides a good indication of the measure of general Latin American support for the extensive claims that have been made. The Principles of Mexico on the Juridical Regime of the Sea declared the old three-mile limit "insufficient" and not a general rule of international law. Each state was declared "competent to establish its territorial waters within reasonable limits." Rights to the continental shelf included "all marine, animal and vegetable species that live in a constant physical and biological relationship with the shelf, not excluding the bethonic species."[28] Needless to say, this rule was intended to accommodate any states, especially Mexico, claiming the right to regulate sedentary fisheries. The right of coastal states to adopt measures of conservation and supervision of living resources beyond their territorial waters was, in the first instance, made subject to the provision that they must not discriminate against foreign fishermen. This limitation was largely negated, however, by the provision that coastal states could claim exclusive rights to "species closely related to the coast, the life of the country, or the needs of the coastal population . . . when the existence of certain species has an important relation to an industry or activity essential to the coastal country." Fifteen Latin American states voted in favor and five abstained.[29]

Much the same position has been supported by most of the Latin American states at general international conferences. In the spring of 1955 an international conference on the technical and scientific aspects of the problem of conserving the living resources of the sea was held in Rome. One of the more controversial proposals made at the conference was contained in a Mexican-Cuban draft. It provided that "where the states concerned have not agreed as to the measures for the conservation of the living resources of the seas, the coastal state may adopt those measures which are based on scientific and technical principles, when the need of conserving these resources becomes imperative. The measures which the coastal state adopts under such conditions must not discriminate against foreign fishermen."[30] During discussions seven Latin American states spoke in support of the provision while two (Panama and Honduras) spoke against it (as did the United States). The provision was narrowly defeated* on the technical grounds that, being juridical in nature, it was outside the competence of the conference. In this vote, however, no Latin American states supported the technical objection—fourteen voted against while two abstained.[31]

The Chilean delegation submitted a similar draft to the seventh session (1955) of the International Law Commission. The essential feature, which authorized unilateral regulation by the coastal state pending agreement with other interested parties, was retained in the I.L.C.'s final draft submitted to the Geneva Conference on the Law of the Sea (1958) and in the convention which that conference produced.

The Geneva Conference on Fishing and Conservation of Living Resources of the High Seas gave a considerable measure of support to some of the Latin American demands. It declared, first of all, that the coastal state has a special interest in the maintenance of the productivity of the living resources of the high seas adjacent to its territory. For this reason it provided that the coastal state may "adopt unilateral measures of conservation . . . in any area of the high seas adjacent to its territorial sea, provided that negotiations to that effect with other states concerned have not led to an agreement within six months."[32] This provision was made subject to the somewhat nebulous requirements that (1) there is urgent need for such measures, (2) they are based on "appropriate scientific findings" and (3) they do not discriminate against foreign fishermen. Finally, if any state objects to these measures, the parties to the convention agree to submit the dispute "for settlement to a special commission of five members, unless the parties agree to such a solution by another method of peaceful settlement, as provided in Article 33 of the Charter of the United Nations."[33] Chile, Ecuador, Costa Rica and Peru had worked for provisions which were even more favorable to the coastal state and would have given it virtually an exclusive and unrestricted right to adopt conservation measures unilaterally.[34] A joint statement by the chairmen of the delegations of Chile, Ecuador and Peru registered their dissatisfaction with the conference measure and declared their intention to uphold the "regional rules" they had proclaimed at Santiago de Chile in 1956[35]—essentially the position of these states discussed in the previous section.

Disagreement between the United States and some Latin American states was also evident in the discussions concerning the continental shelf. The International Law Commission's draft which recognized the

* Twenty-one votes to twenty with three abstentions.

exercise of "sovereign rights" over the continental shelf by the coastal state was objected to by the United States on the grounds that it might become the basis for interference with the freedom of the seas above.[36] A number of Latin American states[37] wanted to make the provision even stronger by substituting the word "sovereignty" for "sovereign rights." There was also disagreement about the nature of the resources of the continental shelf. Mexico, for example, was especially anxious to secure a provision that would recognize her control over shrimp fisheries, or at least not exclude it.

The large number of roll-call votes on the Convention on the Territorial Sea identified more clearly the area and degree of disagreement. Ten Latin American states supported one or another of the various proposals that would have established the breadth of the territorial sea at twelve miles. Three others, Chile, Costa Rica and El Salvador, either abstained or voted against these proposals, apparently not because they extended state jurisdiction too far but because they did not extend it far enough.[38] Thus thirteen Latin American states would appear to support *at least* a twelve-mile limit. Only eight Latin American countries supported the United States compromise proposal of six miles, and two of them (Bolivia and Paraguay) have no seacoast.[39]

A second conference on the law of the sea met at Geneva in 1960 in an attempt to resolve further the conflicting claims regarding the width of the territorial sea and the width and rights in a proposed contiguous and exclusive fishing zone. Thirteen Latin American states supported a compromise proposal put forward by the United States and Canada [40] as amended by Brazil, Cuba and Uruguay.[41] This proposal provided for a six-mile territorial sea, an additional six miles of exclusive fishing rights (subject to certain historic fishing rights for the next ten years) and preferential fishing rights in adjacent areas of the high seas in special situations. A state which felt its fishing rights on the high seas unjustly limited could demand an impartial decision under Article 9 of the 1958 convention.

Last-minute objections by Ecuador and Chile made it impossible to secure the necessary two-thirds majority. Even United States agreement not to press for historic fishing rights within Ecuador's outer six-mile exclusive fishing zone failed to secure the latter's support when the United States delegation could not meet the further demand that all past claims against Ecuador be dropped. The thirteen Latin American states supporting the proposal* included two states which have

* Argentina, Bolivia, Brazil, Colombia, Costa Rica, Cuba, Honduras, Guatemala, Nicaragua, Haiti, The Domincian Republic, Paraguay, Uruguay.

made the more extensive claims (Argentina and Uruguay). A third state (El Salvador) with extensive former claims abstained. Chile, Ecuador, Mexico, Panama and Venezuela voted against the measure.[42]

Nationalism and national interests: low tide for the high seas

A far more exact knowledge of geographic realities, coupled with recent developments in human activities and relationships, has brought into question the old rules concerning coastal waters. New oceanographic explorations and developments have shown the existence of untapped sources of immeasurable wealth in the ocean, its sea bed and subsoil. At the same time population pressure and new demands for a better life by hitherto inarticulate masses have made these resources more important than ever before. The relation between these important social changes and the demands for changes in the rules governing the use of the sea must now occupy our attention.

The surge of twentieth-century nationalism is but one of the many factors related to the unprecedented claims to jurisdiction. One particular aspect of twentieth-century nationalism should be emphasized. It is that aspect which in some areas of the world demands a "just revision" in the relations between colony and mother country, between underdeveloped and industralized states and between small powers and great powers. Although most of Latin America formally threw off colonial rule only a short time after the United States, there is general agreement throughout this area that they have in practice remained under the domination of the great powers, especially the United States.

In the daily press, in more scholarly books and journals and in official government statements, this attitude is unmistakably associated with the demands for new rules governing the use of the sea. All show the conviction that the traditional rules of international law which reserved the maximum of ocean as high seas were rules that grew up in the interest of the great maritime powers. These powers, it is felt, wanted to keep the maximum of sea open to their commerce and industry. They alone had the fishing fleets and protective naval power to permit them to exploit valuable maritime resources thousands of miles from their shores. Since fisheries are most often adjacent to the shore, it was in their interest to limit each state's territorial sea to a minimum and thus permit the maximum opportunity for free exploitation of maritime resources in coastal waters anywhere in the world.

This is but one aspect of the feeling throughout the underdeveloped world that international society has in the past been regulated in the interest of the economically advanced states and that this injustice must be rectified.

The Peruvian delegate, in his statement before the First Committee of the General Assembly, offered the official version of this theme. An appreciable part of international law, he asserted, had in the past been created unilaterally, in the interest of the great powers; some part of international law ought, therefore, to be created through the initiative and action of the small states who invoke natural and legitimate interests, not political and pecuniary ones. He then turned to an argument which has become equally familiar: with the old type of colonial domination over territory disappearing, it would be inadmissable to allow a new type over the high seas even if it is defended in the name of freedom of the seas.[43]

These are arguments that have great appeal in Latin America and the rest of the underdeveloped world. This explains why, even among some of the Latin American states without any direct interest in extending jurisdiction into the high seas, there is considerable support for the extensive claims of other Latin American states.

Needless to say, it is those states whose fishing industry holds the greatest promise who have made the most extensive claims. National fishing interests have developed and of course bring pressure to bear on government policy. But it is not simply the relatively few who are directly connected with fishing industries who matter. More important is the conviction of Latin American nationalists that exploitation of their marine resources may be a significant element in their national economic development. Strongly nationalistic, convinced that economic development holds the key to national salvation, the growing middle sectors thus tend to feel that this is a matter of vital concern.

On this score, at least, there are some statistics to support their assumptions. Between 1948 and 1958 the annual fish catch of Peru increased from 47.7 thousands of metric tons to 750 thousands of metric tons. In the same period the Chilean catch increased from 64.4 thousands of metric tons to 225.8 thousands of metric tons. Mexico showed less spectacular but very significant increase. The Peruvian catch, which amounted to one-third that of the United States, gives some indication of the relative importance of the fishing industry in the Peruvian economy.[44] With one of the richest sources of fish in the world, the Pacific coast countries see this as an important source of future wealth.

When discussing the legality of their claims the Latin American states are somewhat vague. Like the United States claims over the continental shelf, Latin American claims are generally not put forth as being at present a part of international law. Yet it has been asserted in both cases that, in advancing these new claims, the authors are not acting contrary to international law. Ultimately, they argue, the legality of the claims must be judged in terms of their justice and reasonableness in the context of changing conditions.[45] The "justifiable interest" of the coastal state, based on "reasonableness of geographic propinquity" and "necessity," are contrasted by Latin Americans to the "pecuniary interests" of great powers with enormous fishing fleets.

In an effort to show that this position is more than their own concept of "justice," Chile, Ecuador and Peru have tried to establish a scientific base for their view. They have argued that modern biologists and ecologists have shown that extensive complexes of plant and animal life exist within the ocean. The offshore fisheries are thus much affected by what happens much farther out, and in order to protect these fisheries it is necessary to control the more distant activities. These activities are also related to life on the shore.[46]

An important point in Latin American arguments is that their claims to extend jurisdiction into areas of the high seas have a precedent in the policies pursued by other states and especially the United States. While such arguments fail to recognize some important distinctions, they are at least correct in pointing out that the United States too has been willing to extend its jurisdiction when it has been in the national interest to do so.

We have already noted how the United States pressed for Latin American support of the Panama Declaration in 1939, a declaration which clearly limited the rights of belligerent powers in waters until then regarded as high seas. The Peruvian delegate at Geneva in 1958, who as legal adviser to his government had questioned the legality of the declaration, again had occasion to comment on the point: "the great powers which were at present resisting the rights claimed by coastal states had, in fact, during the Second World War, demanded that small countries of Latin America exercise, over a vast sea area rights of jurisdiction and control which included the obstruction of navigation and trade."

Now that the United States is a potential belligerent power, however, it no longer favors any such limitations on access to these waters. The chairman of the United States delegation to the 1958 Geneva Conference has given our present position.

If the territorial sea were extended to twelve miles, any enemy submarine, particularly one with atomic power, which might operate for long periods without surfacing, could operate possibly undetected under waters of a neutral state's territorial sea. But our surface ships could not operate on the surface of these waters within the territorial sea without risking charges of violating such state's neutrality.[47]

The United States doctrine of exclusive rights over the resources of the continental shelf could hardly have been regarded as international law at that time, nor was it defended as such. Yet we made it clear that we intended to act according to the doctrine—law or no law. Infringements on previously established rights on the waters above the continental shelf are inevitable if the resources of the shelf are to be exploited. The delegate from the German Federal Republic pointed to these difficulties at Geneva. "The grant to the coastal state of rights over the continental shelf outside the territorial sea," he said, "raises doubts about possible repercussions of the exercise of these rights on the freedom of the high seas."[48] A member of the United States delegation to the same conference admitted the possibility of a number of such infringements but argued for resolving the problem in favor of the state claiming jurisdiction over the continental shelf.

The representative of the U.S., in supporting the ILC draft of the article, pointed out that Article 70 placed limitations on the freedom to lay submarine cables formulated in Article 27 of the ILC draft; that the 1884 convention for the Protection of Submarine Cables prohibited interference with submarine cables; and that accordingly, some provision was necessary to allow coastal states to take measures for the exploration of the continental shelf which might affect submarine cables. In her view, no more definite criterion than that of reasonableness could be established for the measures which coastal states might take, *for the reason that it was impossible to foresee all the situations that might arise in the application of Article 70.*[49]

There are, perhaps, differences between regulation of travel in certain areas of the high seas, necessitated by mineral exploitating equipment, on the one hand and regulations of fisheries (which may even involve exclusion of foreigners) in the interest of the riparian state on the other. The difference remains to be seen in the extent to which offshore industrial activity will affect these previously established rights.

Perhaps the most balanced judgment on this point is presented by the Cuban jurist, Garcia Amador, who stated that although exploration and exploitation of submarine areas may involve interference with navigation and fishing rights, these rights are not thereby abolished. Under claims to exclusive fishing rights, the rights formerly exercised by other states are abolished. In his opinion, however, the claims to enjoy certain exclusive rights (such as fishing) in areas formerly regarded as high seas are analagous to the rights of the coastal state to the exploration and utilization of the natural resources of its continental shelf.[50]

Changes in the power structure of international society have given a measure of success to these demands for changes in its rules. In the past, a sizable number of great powers who were in general agreement over the advantages of freedom of the seas, at least in time of peace, were able to preserve the integrity of the corresponding rules. But we now have a bipolar power structure, in which one of the two great powers is less concerned over the principle and even sees some immediate advantage in supporting those who are demanding changes. Furthermore, the cold war has intervened to make the use of force or even the use of strong "pressure" inexpedient. Thus the United States seventh fleet protecting United States fishing interests off the coast of Ecuador might well create more problems than it would solve. This fact has permitted small powers to exert a new and far more powerful influence on the rules of international law. Ironically enough, the use of force, which has been ruled out for a great power, has not been ruled out for small powers. Some of the small powers who have been quick to condemn the use of force by great powers have themselves resorted to it to enforce their unilateral proclamations. In 1954, five whaling vessels belonging to A. S. Onassis and flying the Panamanian flag were captured by Peruvian air and naval units. Two were about one hundred and twenty-six miles off the Peruvian coast; three were attacked at distances ranging from three hundred to three hundred and fifty miles off the coast after "hot pursuit" from within the two-hundred-mile zone. The five masters and the owners were ordered to pay a fine of $3,000,000, which they did under a "reservation of further developments." The following year two United States vessels were seized from fourteen to twenty-five miles off the coast of an island belonging to Ecuador. Fines of more than $49,000 were imposed on the two vessels.[51]

The United States as a great maritime power is concerned with preserving a maximum of freedom on the high seas for its commercial vessels. With an important fishing industry it also wishes to preserve the fishing rights which this industry has hitherto enjoyed on the high seas. Most important, security considerations make it essential that its public vessels have a maximum of freedom of operation. Here it finds itself in opposition to a number of Latin American states.

We are, then, quite clearly in a period of significant adjustment of the rules relating to coastal waters. Somewhere among the existing claims new rules will surely emerge. The extensive claims just discussed are far more than mere schemes concocted by a few politicians and legal advisers as moves in the game of power politics. They have their roots both in experiences of the past and in fundamental social and economic changes which are profoundly affecting all of Latin America. Attempts to find a workable set of norms must, therefore, include an awareness of all the social forces that made it necessary to undertake the task in the first place.

Nowhere has the disparity in claims been greater than in the Western Hemisphere. Yet some of the most extensive claims have already been modified considerably, and the Untied States has also given ground on its claims to freedom of the seas. In all of this, various inter-American meetings have played an interesting role. There are certainly indications that they have been used by those states making the most extensive claims as a means of showing Latin American endorsement of their position.[52] At the same time the extremely conciliatory position of Brazil and Colombia, and to some extent Venezuela, are significant. The impressive support which thirteen Latin American states (a fourteenth abstained from voting) at the last Geneva Conference gave to a compromise containing real concessions by the United States is indeed a hopeful sign.

FOOTNOTES

1. L. F. Oppenheim, *International Law: A Treatise* (8th ed. by H. Lauterpacht, London, 1955) vol. I, p. 487. On this question generally, see also C. John Colombos, *The International Law of the Sea* (4th ed., London, 1959), pp. 74 ff.
2. *Amercian State Papers, Foreign Relations*, I, p. 183.
3. P. E. Corbett, *Law in Diplomacy* (Princeton, N.J., 1959), p. 122.
4. 49 *U. S. Statutes at Large*, I, pp. 517 ff.
5. By the second decade of the twentieth century, an increasing number of states began to challenge the three-mile limit. Under the auspices of the League of Nations, an effort was made to reach agreement on some of the conflicting positions with regard to the rules on territorial waters. The Hague Conference for the Codification of International Law, which met in 1930, represented several years of preparatory work and was attended by forty-two participating states and one observer (Russia). On the most difficult and important question, that of the breadth of the territorial sea, it was not pos-

sible to reach an agreement. In view of the significance this question has assumed in inter-American affairs, it comes as something of a surprise to find that only nine Latin American states sent delegates to the conference. Of the six Latin American states represented on the committee that dealt with territorial waters, five favored a six-mile limit and one (Chile) favored a three-mile limit, as did the United States. League of Nations, *Acts of the Conference for the Codification of International Law* (The Hague, 1930), vol. I, Plenary Meetings, pp. 6–13; vol. III, Minutes of the Second Committee: Territorial Waters, pp. 23, 123–125. Even more surprisingly, none of the Latin American states had answered the questions submitted by the Preparatory Committee. Jesse S. Reeves, "The Codification of the Law of Territorial Waters," 24 *AJIL* (1930), p. 492.

6. See Cordell Hull, *Memoirs* (New York, 1948), I, pp. 689 ff.
7. Carnegie Endowment for International Peace, *The International Conferences of American States*, First Supplement, 1933–1944 (Washington, D.C., 1940), pp. 334 ff.
8. P. E. Corbett, *Law and Society in the Relations of States* (New York, 1951), p. 139.
9. Alberto Ulloa, *Informe del Asesor Tecnico Juridico* (Lima, 1941?), p. 443.
10. Hull, *op. cit.*, p. 690.
11. *Ibid.*
12. "Proclamation with Respect to the Natural Resources of the Subsoil and Seabed of the Continental Shelf," Sept. 28, 1945, 10 *Federal Regulations*, p. 12303.
13. "Proclamation with Respect to Coastal Fisheries in Certain Areas of the High Seas," Sept. 28, 1945, 10 *Federal Regulations*, p. 12304.
14. Most of these are contained in United Nations, *Laws and Regulations of the Regime of the Territorial Sea* (1957), U. N. Doc. ST/LEG/SER. B/6. For additional details and comment, see Richard Young, "Recent Developments with Respect to the Continental Shelf," 42 *AJIL* (1948), pp. 849–857; Josef L. Kunz, "Continental Shelf and International Law: Confusion and Abuse," 50 *AJIL* (1956), pp. 828–853; Colombos, *op. cit.*, pp. 84 ff.; Arthur H. Dean, "The Second Geneva Conference on the Law of the Sea: The Fight for Freedom of the Seas," 54 *AJIL* (1960), pp. 751–789.
15. According to the Declaration on the Maritime Zone, Aug. 18, 1952 (Chile, Ecuador and Peru), the parties "proclaim as a principle of international maritime policy that each of them possesses sole sovereignty and jurisdiction over the area of the sea adjacent to the coast of its own country and extending not less than 200 nautical miles from the said coast." U. N. Doc. ST/LEG/SER. B/6, pp. 723–724.
16. U. N. Docs. A/C.6/SR. 486, at 28, 29; A/C.6/SR. 489, at 43, 45; A/C.6/SR. 496 at 84, 86; A/C.6/SR. 498, at 97 (1956).
17. Kunz, *op. cit.*, pp. 836 ff.
18. The Society of Comparative Legislation and International Law, *The Law of the Sea* (London, 1958), pp. 36–42.
19. Inter-American Juridical Committee, *Draft Convention on Territorial Waters and Related Questions* (Washington, 1952).
20. *Ibid.*
21. *Ibid.*, pp. 10–19.

22. Inter-American Council of Jurists, Second Meeting, *Handbook* (Washington, D.C., 1953), pp. 31–38.
23. Resolution XIX.
24. Inter-American Council of Jurists, Second Meeting, Report of the *Executive Secretary*, pp. 24–26.
25. Kunz, *op. cit.*, pp. 835–836. The three powers met again in Lima, in 1954, after the seizure of the Onassis whalers by Peru. Here they reaffirmed the two-hundred mile principle and pledged to assist one another if they became involved in international litigation relating to this principle. In 1955, the three powers met jointly with the United States in an attempt to resolve some of the differences in their position and that of the United States. Here Chile, Ecuador and Peru held firmly to the position they had taken in 1952, and none of the differences were actually resolved. See U.S. Department of State, *Santiago Negotiations on Fishery Conservation Problems* (1955).
26. Inter-American Specialized Conference on "Conservation of Natural Resources; the Continental Shelf and Marine Waters," Ciudad Trujillo, March 15–28, 1956, *Final Act.*
27. *Ibid.*
28. Resolution XIII, *Final Act.*
29. The Dominican Republic, Colombia, Bolivia, Guatemala and Nicaragua abstained. Although Brazil voted for the resolution, her reservation seemed to negate this position. The United States voted against the resolution. See *Final Act.*
30. Doc. A/CONF. 10/GC.1/Rev.1.
31. See Record of the Twenty-First Plenary Meeting, pp. 17–18.
32. Article 7.
33. Article 9.
34. Doc. A/CONF. 13/C.3/L.41.
35. Doc. A/CONF. 13/L.50.
36. Doc. A/CONF. 13/C.4/SR. 20.
37. Argentina, Venezuela, Peru, Guatemala and Chile.
38. Summary Records of the First Committee, pp. 177–178.
39. *Ibid.*, p. 180.
40. Doc. A/CONF. 19/C.1/L.10.
41. Doc. A/CONF. 19/L.4 and Annex.
42. Doc. A/CONF. 19/SR. 13, at p. 8.
43. See *Revista Peruana de Derecho Internacional*, XVIII (Jan.–June, 1958), pp. 16 ff. For similar arguments presented by the Ecuadoran delegate see United Nations, General Assembly, Sixth Committee, *Verbatim Records*, p. 155.
44. United Nations, *Statistical Yearbook* for 1957, table 34; for 1959, table 37.
45. See reference to "The Legal System" by F. V. Garcia Amador, *The Exploitation and Conservation of the Resources of the Sea* (Leyden, 1959), p. 202. At times, however, the arguments have seemed to insist that the substance of their claims has already become a part of international law. See Kunz, *op. cit.*; J. L. de Azcárraga de Bustamante, *La plataforma submarina y el derecho internacional* (Madrid, 1952); Enrique Garcia Sayan, *Notas sobre la soberania marítima de Peru, Defensa de la 200 millas de mar peruano ante*

las recientes transgresiones (Lima, 1953). As noted, however, official position has retreated from this extreme.

46. Henry Reiff, *The United States and the Treaty Law of the Sea* (Minneapolis, 1959), p. 308.

47. Arthur H. Dean, "The Geneva Conference on the Law of the Sea; What was Accomplished," 52 *AJIL* (1958), pp. 610–611.

48. Marjorie M. Whiteman, "Conference on the Law of the Sea: The Continental Shelf," 52 *AJIL* (1958), p. 637.

49. *Ibid.*, p. 642. Author's italics.

50. Garcia Amador, *op. cit.*, pp. 67 ff., 95, 202.

51. Kunz, *op. cit.*, pp. 836 ff.

52. Richard Young, "Pan American Discussions on Offshore Claims," 50 *AJIL* (1956), p. 913.

Chapter Seven

European Colonies
and "Occupied Territories"

Historical setting

European colonies and possessions in the New World are a matter of immediate conflict for only two Latin American states—Argentina claims the British-held Falkland Islands, and Guatemala claims British Honduras.* The Argentines and the Guatemalans refer to these as "occupied territories" and have succeeded in having this terminology adopted by recent inter-American conferences and meetings. Chile has also classified British claims in the Antarctic as "occupied territories," but these will be discussed in the following chapter. The remaining European possessions† are generally referred to as such or as "European colonies." In the following discussion these two more common terms will be used in referring to all territories held by European powers, thus dropping the distinction of "occupied territories."

Although the remaining European possessions are of little real value to anyone, they have created problems in inter-American relations and have the potential for creating more problems in the future. They have been the subject of considerable debate at two general inter-American conferences and at one specialized conference since World

---

* Argentines refer to the Falkland Islands as "the Malvinas'" and Guatemalans refer to British Honduras as "Belice."

† British Guiana, the West Indies, Bahamas, Bermuda, French Guiana, Martinique, Guadeloupe and dependencies, Dutch Guiana (Surinam) and the Netherlands Antilles.

War II. The conflicts and discussions that have centered around these possessions demonstrate the complex political, emotional and historical factors that condition attitudes toward rules of interstate conduct.

The impetus which has from time to time made colonies and colonialism an issue in inter-American affairs has always come from the states whose national interests were directly affected. The first pronouncement on colonies in the New World was of course the Monroe Doctrine, which was clearly a statement of United States national interest. This was intended purely as an instrument of national policy and not as a charter for concerted hemispheric action. It only stated in advance that the United States would be opposed to any extension of the European system or any *further* colonization in this hemisphere. This view happened to coincide with the interests of the new Latin American republics, where its reception was universally favorable.

But in time much resentment was to grow out of the Monroe Doctrine, a development which today helps condition Latin American attitudes toward the question of colonies. There were a number of times in the first half of the nineteenth century when Latin American states invoked the Doctrine, for protection against intervention or other pressures from European powers, but received no assistance from the United States. Certainly more irritating to Latin Americans was the fact that the United States soon reserved for itself the right to do the very things that it insisted Europe could not do. The conquest of nearly one-half of the territory of Mexico, military intervention in Central America and the Caribbean and, eventually, more subtle forms of pressure convinced them that United States imperialism had been substituted for European.

The first collective action on the question of colonies was taken during World War II, under strong pressure from the United States.[1] With the fall of France and the Low Countries, the United States feared that England might occupy the French and Dutch colonies in this hemisphere and that conflict with Germany would follow. At the Second Meeting of the Ministers of Foreign Affairs of the American Republics, held at Havana in 1940, she thus urged the Latin American republics to join in a declaration which would state the intention of all American states to prevent any such conflicts from arising.

Argentina took the leadership in opposing this declaration on the grounds that there was no legal basis for such action, that it would be a warlike act and would leave states like Argentina with long seacoasts open to attack, and that the United States would be unable to offer adequate protection. According to Secretary of State Hull, another group of delegates offered this argument: "Your Government sends you down here to commit us to what we've sworn we would never agree to on account of its many abuses—and that's the Monroe Doctrine."[2] But strong pressure by the United States, which was then more concerned with security than legality, was enough to gain the approval of the desired measure.

It was finally agreed that whenever any of the European possessions in the Americas might be in danger "of becoming a subject of barter of territory or change of sovereignty," the American states might set up a regime of provisional administration for the territory involved. Eventually, the territories would be returned to their previous status or organized as autonomous states, "whichever of these alternatives shall appear the more practicable and just."[3] It was, therefore, somewhat more than a mere "holding" measure, since it clearly indicated the possibility of interference with the sovereignty of the mother countries if this should "appear the more practicable and just." As a wartime measure no one seems to have been very much concerned with its legality. As things turned out, the Act of Havana never had to be applied. Hitler made no attempt to assume sovereignty over the European possessions or to transfer them to anyone else.

The next time that colonies became an issue in inter-American relations, it was on the initiative of Argentina and Guatamala. The British-Argentine dispute over the Falkland Islands and the British-Guatemalan dispute over British Honduras had been in existence for well over a century. As had been true of United States maneuvers at Havana, both Argentina and Guatemala had a specific national interest in mind for which they hoped to enlist the support of the other American states.

The Falkland Islands (Malvinas)

Disagreement still prevails over who discovered the Falkland Islands, although the Spanish probably had the more valid claims.[4] Whoever it was, a British settlement was made there in 1765 but was abolished by the Spanish in 1770. The following year an agreement was reached by which possession of Port Egmont was restored to the British but only upon the latter's promise of speedy abandonment, a promise which was carried out by 1774. After this date the British never again occupied any of the territory until after Spanish power had been withdrawn from South America. "Subsequent to the British abandonment of Port Egmont . . . the Spanish exercised the fullest sovereignty over the whole group of islands, not limiting their acts of government and control to the islands themselves, but extending their power over the surrounding areas."[5] These acts appear at no time to have been disputed and seemed to receive the formal approval of Great Britain in the Nootka Sound Convention, which recognized the *status quo* in the southern half of South America.[6]

After the Argentine Declaration of Independence in 1816, the islands became a part of the new republic (The United Provinces of La Plata), but the colonists had been withdrawn since the 1810 revolt against the Bonapartist regime. In the next years, the La Plata states had far too many problems at home to concern themselves with the islands; thus formal possession was not taken until 1820. From this time on, however, various real acts of sovereignty took place (such as enforcement of fishing regulations, appointment of a governor and granting of land concessions). The first British protest against these acts was made in 1829, claiming the islands as British, but no action was taken.[7]

In 1831, the Governor of the islands seized some United States vessels for ignoring Argentine fishing decrees, and in the ensuing controversy he himself was taken prisoner on board a United States warship. It was at this point that Great Britain decided to enforce her claims and occupied the islands, with the tacit approval of the United States. In the course of the controversy, the United States conveniently insisted that the islands were never Spanish or Argentine but were in fact British.[8] This opportunistic action was soon regretted. In 1853, when the United States–British struggle for hegemony in this hemisphere became acute, our vessels were again seized, off the Falkland Islands, this time by the British. Then we conveniently took the opposite view, arguing that the question of sovereignty had never been settled.[9]

According to the most careful study of this whole controversy, British occupation could hardly have been regarded as anything but outright seizure of territory. "The right of the Argentine nation to stand in the place of Spain with reference to the sovereignty over the Falklands was established by the successful revolution, and by the assertion and maintenance of sovereignty over the Falklands as against Spain."[10] Argentina has issued periodic protests over British occupation and thus continues to claim sovereignty. Great Britain now claims title by prescription, which Argentina in turn denies, on the grounds that forceful occupation in the presence of formal protest is invalid.

Although both parties have stated their claims in legal terminology, neither has shown any interest in submitting the question to adjudication.

British Honduras (Belize)

Great Britain's first interest in the area now called British Honduras began in the seventeenth century with the unauthorized ventures of British buccaneers who began to cut logwood along the coast, then clearly recognized as Spanish territory. By the Treaty of Paris (1763) Great Britain received formal acknowledgment of these rights, but the same treaty carefully reserved Spanish sovereignty over the area. Later treaties, the last in 1814, reaffirmed this sovereignty in unambiguous terms.[11]

Toward the end of the eighteenth century Spanish administration made some changes which were later to complicate matters. Until this time the area had been under the old Presidency of Guatemala. In about 1787 it was apparently transferred to the Captaincy General of Yucatan, which was under the Viceroyalty of New Spain (Mexico). At this time the British concession only went as far south as the Sibun River (see map), and this was the area transferred to the Captaincy General of Yucatan. After 1814 the British settlers moved south of the Sibun River and into territory clearly under the jurisdiction of the old Presidency of Guatemala.[12]

In the 1820's, Spanish authority in Mexico and Central America was replaced by successful revolutions, but Britain continued to occupy her concessions and regarded Spain as the rightful soverign over them.[13] Guatemala also regarded herself as the rightful successor to Spanish sovereignty in the area and, under the principle of *uti possidetis*, claimed the entire area occupied by Britain. This principle originally provided that at the conclusion of peace, in the absence of any express stpulation, the belligerents would hold title to territory under their control.[14] It was later applied by Latin American states in their boundary disputes to mean that the old Spanish administrative boundaries would remain as the boundaries between them. Although this version of the principle has been widely applied by Latin American states, it has never been accepted as a general rule of international law. Even among Latin American states its usefulness has been limited by the vagueness of the old Spanish boundaries.[15] Furthermore, Guatemala has never been able to explain how, even under the principle of

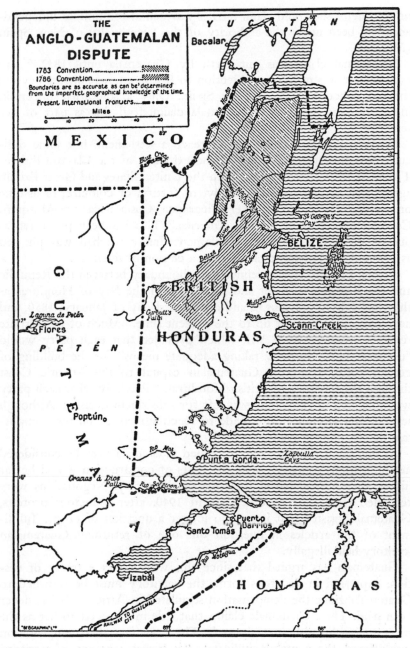

Source: R. A. Humphreys, "The Anglo-Guatemalan Dispute," *International Affairs*, 24 (1948), p. 388.

uti possidetis, she could claim territory which at the time of independence had been under the authority of the Viceroyalty of New Spain (Mexico).

No formal claim was put forth by Guatemala until 1832,[16] and even then it was mainly an objection to British encroachments beyond the old concessions granted by Spain. Only a somewhat uncertain indication was given that Guatemala claimed all this as part of her territory.[17]

By 1859 Britain was anxious to reach a settlement, but some difficulty was anticipated because of the existence of the Clayton-Bulwer Treaty of 1850. By this treaty both the United States and Great Britain agreed that neither would "occupy, or fortify, or colonize; or assume or exercise any dominion over Nicaragua, Costa Rica, the Mosquito Coast, or any part of Central America." This has been put forth as one of the reasons why the settlement finally reached was phrased as a boundary settlement rather than a cession of territory.

Article I of this treaty defined "the boundary between the Republic and the British settlement and possession in the Bay of Honduras as they had existed previous to and on the first day of January, 1850, and have continued to exist up to the present time." Much of the dispute revolves around Article VII, which provided that each party would "use their best efforts by taking adequate means" for the building of certain roads, from the Guatemalan capital to the Atlantic Coast through the territory of British Honduras.[18] Precisely what each party was obligated to contribute was left for subsequent decision. Although several later attempts were made to reach agreement on these important details, none proved successful.

At one point Great Britain informed Guatemala that she considered her obligations canceled, since the costs of construction would be far higher than anticipated at the time of the treaty. Negotiations were reopened from time to time, but in 1940, after numerous protests, Guatemala insisted that it was no longer a question of proper fulfillment of the articles in question but one of returning Guatemalan territory held illegally.

Guatemala has argued that since this was in fact a treaty of cession, expressed in decorous form, the territory must be returned to Guatemala, since the compensation stipulated in Article VII has never been paid. Thus, Guatemala claims that title must revert to her as the successor to Spanish sovereignty.[19] The very fact that compensation was offered, she contends, indicates that it was a cession of territory and not simply a boundary settlement. Britain claims that the treaty was a genuine boundary settlement, as the letter of the document suggests, and therefore only confirmed British sovereignty.[20] The real nature of the Treaty of 1859 is clearly the fundamental question.

Evidence recently uncovered shows that the negotiators, and apparently their governments, did in fact regard the treaty as a cession of territory for which compensation was to be paid.[21] But a further complicating factor is the fact that the amount of compensation was indicated only in secret agreements of undetermined validity. The shady situation is well described in these words.

The British negotiator delayed informing his government of the full meaning of his private, unwritten understanding with the Guatemalan representative. Acting thus in ignorance, the British government interpreted Article VII in a way highly offensive to Guatemala. A British representative then withheld this interpreation from Guatemalan ears until the treaty passed an important political test. Even then certain elements of the Guatemalan government, fearing repudiation of both the treaty and themselves, kept the unfavorable interpretation a closely guarded secret. In this they were encouraged by the British negotiator.[22]

This being the case, is the British government responsible for nonfulfillment of Article VII, and is the entire convention therefore void? Guatemala answers both these questions in the affirmative, and Great Britain answers in the negative.

Guatemala contends that, the treaty being void, the territory must revert to Guatemala as the successor to Spanish sovereignty. Great Britain contends that even if the treaty of 1859 were now void, Guatemala was never the rightful possessor of sovereignty over the area. In the first place, a large part of it was under the Captaincy General of Yucatan, ultimately under New Spain, and thus Guatemala could not inherit this sovereignty even if the principle of *uti possidetis* were valid (which Britain does not admit). In the second place, Britain continued to occupy the territory after the departure of Spanish authority and has continued to do so ever since. Guatemala in turn claims that occupation, in the presence of formal Guatemalan protests, does not establish a valid claim.

Although Britain and Mexico have, by treaty, settled title to the territory formerly under the Captaincy General of Yucatan, Mexico has insisted that if Britain relinquishes her rights in the area, it must revert to Mexico. Thus Mexico and Guatemala also have conflicting claims.

In 1880, Guatemala proposed arbitration by the head of some

friendly state,[23] but the offer was rejected by Great Britain.[24] In 1937, Guatemala again proposed arbitration, this time by the President of the United States. Again Great Britain rejected the offer but, at the same time, proposed that the question be submitted to the Permanent Court of International Justice at The Hague. Guatemala rejected this on the grounds that "the questions at issue are not only of a juridical order and therefore depart from the somewhat rigid regulations of that tribunal, which is exclusively *de jure*, with strict legal rules to which it must adhere in its decisions."[25] Nearly all of these are questions which are anything but clear under international law.

In 1946, the British government offered to submit the dispute to the International Court of Justice and did so in terms which would seem to be broad enough to cover not only the treaty rights and obligations but also legal rights not based on treaty. It declared that it would accept "the jurisdiction of the Court in all legal disputes concerning the interpretation, application or validity of any treaty relating to the boundaries of British Honduras, and over any such questions arising out of any conclusions which the court may reach with regard to such treaty."[26] Although Guatemala has insisted all along that the law was on her side, she agreed to accept the offer only if the dispute should be settled *ex aequo et bono* and not on a strictly legal basis.[27]

Resort to the inter-American system

Unable to gain satisfaction for their claims through bilateral negotiations, Argentina and Guatemala have sought to enlist the support of the other American states. In this they have been able to draw on the strong feelings of anticolonialism (or anti-imperialism) which prevail throughout Latin America. Thus any crusade against any form of foreign domination is likely to receive the warm support of most Latin American governments. To the extent that it might be possible to establish the general principle that colonial rule is contrary to basic principles of this hemisphere, the specific interests of Argentina and Guatemala would be served. At the request of Guatemala, the question of European colonies in America was included on the agenda of the Ninth International Conference of American States, held at Bogotá in 1948.

It was clear from the outset that this would be a purely political treatment of the subject. The one case of colonialism for which an inter-American organization could best claim jurisdiction—Puerto Rico —was by clear implication excluded. References, in debates and draft resolutions, were to European colonies or to control by an extra-continental or non-continental power.[28] This, naturally, was a bid for United States support, for each nation realized that such support was essential for the success of the whole move.

It was equally clear that the case would be one-sided. The Argentine delegate objected in committee to the fact that the British Embassy in Bogotá had circulated, via the secretariat, its position on the controversies with Argentina and Guatemala. He asked for an agreement that this should be prohibited in the future.[29]

The United States delegate alluded to this curious situation, noting that there had been submitted historical, geographic and legal data which would give the impression that this was a court of justice. Yet, he said, if such were within the jurisdiction of the committee, principles of law and justice would demand that the other party or parties be heard. Thus, he continued, the United States could not accept any resolution which might appear as prejudging the controversies of friendly nations.[30]

The Argentine delegate made it clear that his draft declaration was intended to provide a legal foundation for Argentine claims.

For this very reason we have presented a project for a declaration, through which we affirm that it is the just aspirations of the peoples and of the governments of the American republics that the colonialism or *de facto* occupation which exists in America be terminated and that the rights and responsibilities growing out of the declaration, and the juridical titles which the American republics possess, give rights, responsibilities and titles with respect to foreign nations occupying the continent.[31]

He then implied that if Argentine cooperation on other issues was to be expected, American support for Argentina's position was vital.

Consequently, Mr. President, we come to this conference to demand American solidarity. American solidarity is like loyalty: it is the only thing that joins the hearts. We hope with profound faith that this conference will lend us its full solidarity in this problem. If this were not to be, Argentine faith in American unity and solidarity would be absolutely broken. Our profound faith in the law would be broken; perhaps the spirit of unity and solidarity which Argentina practices would be broken. But I am certain that this will not happen. Never when the American countries have asked for solidarity have the rest of the countries withheld it.[32]

The Guatemalan delegate spoke in terms that would certainly appeal to Latin American nationalism. More than the interests of Guatemala and Argentina were at stake. Guatemala considered that America had arrived at full political maturity and had a right to be respected by extracontinental powers. If colonialism was crumbling in Asia and Africa, the colonial powers should understand that America would, with as much or more reason, vindicate its sovereignty.[33]

As has often happened, the most carefully reasoned exposition was presented by the delegate from Brazil. He first turned to the supposed precedent which had been set by the Act of Havana, concerning the provisional administration of European colonies and possessions in the Americas. This act, he felt, could hardly be considered a valid precedent inasmuch as it was issued in 1940, when two colonial powers were occupied by the enemy and the third struggled alone. Furthermore, the act did not question coloninal sovereignty; it only prepared for the eventuality that sovereignty might change hands.

As far as the "occupied" American territories were concerned, Brazil felt that the conference could do no more than express its hope for a friendly settlement without usurping a jurisdiction it clearly did not have. As far as colonies were concerned, Brazil too hoped they could have self-government.

But how is that desire to be achieved? Can it be affirmed here that any of those territories now have, at the present time, the political, economic and social conditions in order to live by themselves and govern themselves? In this campaign for the suppression of colonial rule in America, what is desired and what is sought for is the political emancipation of non-sovereign people; because I assume that no one here is thinking of substituting himself for the European powers in the administration of such territories. If that is the case . . . how can we, men of responsibility, pretend to advance a simple solution to a problem, contingent in its very nature, without measuring the consequences which are derived from it.

Finally he reminded the delegates that Chapter XI of the United Nations Charter was not a dead letter and that the world organization was the only proper forum for a question involving non-American states. This inter-American conference, continuing its task of perfecting the juridical bases of inter-American life, should give the world the impression that it adopts the same criteria in its relation with the rest of the world.[34]

The delegate from the Dominican Republic also insisted that the organization lacked jurisdiction, but he and the delegates from Brazil and the United States were the only ones who seem to have been in the least concerned with this legal problem. Chile was willing to go along with the declaration but opposed creation of the Committee on Dependent Territories "because it would serve no useful purpose and might, on the contrary, bring on practical inconveniences." The verbatim records of the steering committee (on which all states are represented) show that the questions raised by Brazil and the United States were simply ignored.[35]

The resolution which was finally approved declared "that it is a just aspiration of the American Republics that colonialism and the occupation of American territories by extracontinental countries should be brought to an end" and resolved "to create an American Committee on Dependent Territories to centralize the study of the problem of the existence of dependent and occupied territories, in order to find an adequate solution to that question."[36] Thus at least the second paragraph of the Argentine declaration had been dropped ("that the rights and responsibilities emergent from this declaration, and the juridical titles which the American republics possess, give rights, responsibilities and titles with respect to foreign occupying nations"). Brazil, the Dominican Republic and the United States abstained from voting on the resolution, for reasons already indicated. Chile approved the declaratory paragraph but abstained with respect to the establishment of the committee.[37]

An American Committee on Dependent Territories was accordingly created and held its first and only meeting at Havana in 1949. Fourteen Latin American countries were represented (no delegations were sent by Bolivia, Brazil, Chile, the Dominican Republic, Nicaragua, Uruguay and the United States).[38] Lengthy discussions arose over whether or not the committee was competent to take up the case of Puerto Rico. But the uncertainty on this question did not prevent the Committee from devoting nearly one-third of its report to blistering attacks by the Independence and Nationalist parties of Puerto Rico against United States imperialism, its continued military intervention and the horrible plight of Puerto Ricans.[39] Nor was any apparent notice taken of the fact that during the conference the senate of Puerto Rico adopted a unanimous resolution censuring the action of the Committee and declared that Puerto Rico had the opportunity and would make its own decision on its future relationship with the United States.[40] The final resolution of the Committee declared that "given the present economic, political and social situation in Puerto Rico, the committee hopes that this nation will have an opportunity to express itself definitively and freely so as to decide its own destiny."[41]

On the question of dependent territories there was really little that could be done. A flat demand for a particular course of action by the colonial powers would run the risk of demonstrating impotence. The resolution adopted therefore merely requested the cooperation of non-American countries "to the end that their American colonies and possessions may be established as independent states or placed under the trusteeship system of administration, in conformity with the Charter of the United Nations."[42]

Real difficulties developed over the question of "occupied territories" (British Honduras and the Falkland Islands). To a proposed resolution that called upon Great Britain to submit the question of British Honduras to a decision *ex aequo et bona* by the International Court of Justice, Mexico insisted on adding a provision reserving her right to intervene with regard to her claim over the area bordering on Yucatan. Guatemala was unwilling to accept this and, with the support of Honduras, El Salvador and Costa Rica (Panama abstaining), was able to defeat the Mexican proposal.[43]

At this point the Mexican delegate informed his colleagues that he would take a page from the book on cold war politics and withdraw from the Committee.[44] The Committee finally had to settle for a compromise "agreement" and "resolution." The "agreement" called for a peaceful settlement of the issue and for the sending of reports and communications to the next meeting of ministers of foreign affairs or to the next international conference of American states. The "resolution" could only (1) reiterate the desire of America to resolve the colonial problem, (2) note that the Committee had knowledge of the claims to sovereignty over territories occupied by Great Britain and that these should be resolved peacefully and (3) note "that all legitimate and just claims of any American state should have the solidarity of the other American republics."[45]

The proceedings show no evidence of discussion of the practical gain for the American states which presumably would result from having the more advanced British, French and Dutch colonies established as independent and democratic states. It simply was not seriously considered, as far as the records indicate. Nor was there any discussion of the fact that the more backward colonies might continue in much the same condition if they were to be converted into trust territories with the same mother countries acting as administering authorities. "What the committee sought to do was to proclaim a principle, and thus gain indirect support for the position it was to take in the matter of occupied territories."[46]

The Tenth Inter-American Conference received the report of the Committee and produced three new resolutions. One of them, submitted by Argentina, merely reiterated the principles set forth in the earlier resolution.[47] Another, submitted by Brazil, called upon the extracontinental powers with colonies in this hemisphere not to delay in carrying out the principles put forth in the United Nations Charter with respect to self-determination of peoples under colonial rule.[48] The part of the Brazilian proposal that had called upon the colonial powers to place under the United Nations trusteeship system any colonies not ready for independence failed by a margin of one vote.[49] The last resolution, submitted by Ecuador, recommended to the Council of the O.A.S. that it convoke the American Committee on Dependent Territories "when circumstances make this advisable."[50] No further meetings of the Committee had been called as of 1962.

Colonialism versus "American principles"

Although the Argentine and Guatemalan claims are phrased in legal language, and although it is argued that international law is on their side, neither one now shows any disposition to submit its dispute to an impartial judicial decision. Guatemala has done so on condition that it be decided *ex aequo et bono*, a condition which Great Britain has not been willing to accept. The reason given by Guatemala for her refusal of a purely judical settlement was that she regarded a settlement *ex aequo et bono* as "the only possible way of resolving this painful question in a cordial, just and equitable way."[51] Guatemala fears that under existing international law Great Britain has the better case *on strictly legal grounds*. Britain's long occupation, although contested, might be considered as giving legal title, and the treaty of 1859 might well be taken at its face value, leaving Britain with an obligation to fulfill compensations. But it is felt that such a conclusion follows the old international law based on the will of the strong, thus explaining the dual approach of pressing for inter-American resolutions supporting Argentine and Guatemalan claims on the one hand, and appeals to "American international law" on the other.[52]

The question of European possessions, like the question of territorial waters, reveals a general Latin American attitude toward the formation of regional norms of interstate conduct. There is a tendency to feel that the American states have a right to order their affairs within this hemisphere according to their mutual needs and interests, even to the detriment of established rights of non-American states. A color of legality is provided by declarations and resolutions which presumably state certain "American principles" or "American rules of law" and whose sanction is the approval of a majority of American states. Anti-colonial feeling has apparently been strong enough to permit Latin Americans to forget about their traditional sensitivity on the question of intervention.

It is important to remember that, to Latin Americans, opposition to continued colonial occupation of territories in this hemisphere is part of a far more momentous "crusade." Not only is it seen as an inseparable part of a general and all-important struggle for genuine independence, but it also provides a concrete and clearcut object to focus upon in a campaign in which the related "evils" are less easily proved. Many Latin Americans seem little concerned about the right of self-determination as opposed to the right of independence. Many of them refuse to recognize the right of Surinam to remain as an autonomous, but not independent, member of the Kingdom of the Netherlands. They also refuse to recognize the right of Puerto Rico to be an *Estado Libre Asociado* instead of an independent republic.

A fairly typical attitude is expressed in these lines.

Since the beginning of the 19th Century, Latin America has sustained its will to be independent. The decision to end all forms of colonial rule began a process, for that very reason called "decolonization," which has animated the struggle against economic imperialism. . . . For him who does not see the historical process as one simply of events, "decolonization" has many shadings. . . . This movement ranges from territorial questions to more subtle propositions of cultural autonomy.[53]

In spite of this "regional outlook," however, it must be admitted that the Latin American handling of the problem of European pos-sessions has been neither extreme nor uncompromising. Although a majority of Latin American states have generally supported Argentina and Guatemala, they have not supported the more extreme resolutions these two have desired. To this extent, the rest of the Latin American states have served as a restraining influence. The Mexican-Guatemalan dispute over a portion of British Honduras of course precluded a united front and, if nothing else, serves to demonstrate that the ques-tion is not entirely one of imperialism versus American law and justice.

Should disorders develop within the European possessions, attitudes in the Latin American countries might well become more extreme. The social revolutionary movements which are gaining momentum throughout the area will be far more outspoken against all forms of colonialism. Even the most conservative governments have found it convenient to appeal to nationalist sentiment by endorsing the statements and declarations we have reviewed.

The issue is complicated for the United States by its wider security interests. The states whose colonialism was condemned are her principal allies in the cold war. For this reason even the technique of carefully limiting resolutions to the colonialism of non-American states could not enlist the support of the United States. Of concern also was the fact that difficult and embarrassing discussion on Puerto Rico and the Panama Canal would inevitably arise.

Anti-Yankee elements in Latin America can and do use the issue as a means of showing the United States in an unfavorable light. It serves as a convenient demonstration of where United States sentiments lie—with its Latin American neighbors or its imperial allies in Europe. At least some Latin Americans feel the latter have taken precedence.

[The United States] has no immediate interest, because to support this question, it would oppose the colonial interests of England, France and Holland; nations important in the North Atlantic Defense Pact. Besides . . . the American Committee on Dependent Territories could also serve as an instrument for recommending the independence of Puerto Rico.[54]

[The new movement for liberation] does not gain much force, due to the political and economic influence which these nations [England, France and Holland] exercise on the governments of the ex-Hispanic colonies and to the complicity of United States imperialism.[55]

FOOTNOTES

1. Cordell Hull, *Memoirs* (New York, 1948), I, pp. 823 ff.
2. *Ibid.*, p. 824.
3. Ministers of Foreign Affairs of the American Republics, Second Meeting, *Report* (1940), p. 38.
4. Julius Goebel, Jr., *The Struggle for the Falkland Islands* (New Haven, 1927), chapter 2.
5. *Ibid.*, p. 432.
6. *Ibid.*
7. Daniel Antokoletz, *Tratado de derecho internacional público* (Buenos Aires, 1925), II, pp. 170–171.
8. *Ibid.*, p. 174.
9. J. B. Moore, *Digest*, I, p. 888.
10. Goebel, *op. cit.*, p. 468.

11. Guatemala, Ministry of Foreign Affairs, *White Book*, the Belize Question (1938). Two very excellent short accounts are available: R. A. Humphreys, "The Anglo-Guatemalan Dispute," *International Affairs*, 24 (1948), pp. 387–404; and L. M. Bloomfield, *The British Honduras–Guatemala Dispute* (Toronto, 1958).
12. Humphreys, *op. cit.*, pp. 389–390.
13. *Ibid.*, p. 391.
14. William E. Hall, *A Treatise on International Law* (8th ed. by Pearce Higgins, 1924), p. 673.
15. L. Podestá-Costa, *op. cit.*, I, pp. 184–185.
16. *Ibid.*, p. 40; Bloomfield, *op. cit.*, p. 14. In 1837, a Guatemalan cruiser had been sent to the area south of the Sibun River to drive away a British ship navigating in the area, *White Book*, p. 40.
17. *White Book*, p. 40.
18. *Ibid.*, pp. 103 ff.
19. A convenient summary of the Guatemalan position may be found in Guatemala, Ministerio de Relaciones Exteriores, *Puntos capitales que sostiene el gobierno de Guatemala* (1945). It will be found in more detailed form in the *White Book* and *Supplements*. Convenient non-official sources are Bloomfield, *op. cit.*; Humphreys, *op. cit.*; and Joseph L. Kunz, "Guatemala vs. Great Britain: in re Belice," 40 *AJIL* (1946), pp. 383–390.
20. A good summary of the British position may be found in *The British Yearbook of International Law*, 1947, XXIV, pp. 406 ff.; Kunz, *op. cit.*; Bloomfield, *op. cit.*; Humphreys, *op. cit.*
21. Wayne M. Clegern, "New Light on the Belize Dispute," 52 *AJIL* (1958), pp. 280–297.
22. *Ibid.*, p. 294.
23. *White Book*, p. 335.
24. *Ibid.*, p. 338.
25. *Ibid.*, p. 429.
26. *British Yearbook of International Law*, 1947, XXIV, p. 408.
27. Guatemala, Secretaria de Relaciones Exteriores, *La Controversia sobre Belice durante el año de 1945* (1946).
28. International Conference of American States, Ninth, *Actas y documentos*, II, pp. 259 ff.
29. *Ibid.*, pp. 61 ff.
30. *Ibid.*, pp. 296–297.
31. *Ibid.*, p. 265.
32. *Ibid.* p. 265.
33. *Ibid.*, p. 303.
34. *Ibid.*, pp. 294–296.
35. *Ibid.*, pp. 263–304.
36. Resolution XXXIII, *Final Act.*
37. International Conference of American States, Ninth, *Actas y documentos*, II, p. 338.
38. American Committee on Dependent Territories, *Memoria*, p. 16.
39. American Committee on Dependent Territories, *Informe.*
40. *Inter-American Juridical Yearbook, 1950–1951*, p. 118.
41. American Committee on Dependent Territories, *Informe*, p. 459.

42. *Ibid.*, pp. 338–339.
43. *Ibid.*, pp. 348–349.
44. *Ibid.*, p. 349.
45. *Ibid.*, p. 450.
46. *Inter-American Juridical Yearbook, 1950–1951*, p. 116.
47. Resolution XCVI, *Final Act.*
48. Resolution XCVII, *Final Act.*
49. *Report of the Delegation of the United States*, p. 10.
50. Resolution XCVIII, *Final Act.*
51. Guatemala, Secretaria de Relaciones Exteriores, *La controversia sobre Belice durante el año 1945*, p. 41.
52. See, for example, Miguel Angel Campa, "Reivindicaciones territoriales de América," *Revista de derecho internacional*, LIII (Havana, June 1948), pp. 163–187.
53. Manuel Moreno Sánchez, "El imperialismo en América Latina," *Cuadernos Americanos*, XL (July–Aug. 1948), p. 62.
54. Antonio Linares Fleytas, "El problema de las colonias y territorios dependientes de naciones europeas en América," *Revista de derecho internacional*, LV (Havana, Jan.–June 1949), pp. 48–49.
55. *Ibid.*, p. 45.

Chapter Eight

Antarctic Claims

The significance of the Antarctic

It has now become fairly standard practice in diplomatic intercourse to define the Antarctic as the area south of 60° south latitude, including all ice shelves.[1] This includes the entire Antarctic continent and most of the islands of the area but excludes the high seas. In the following pages, we shall confine ourselves primarily to a consideration of the claims to that part of the Antarctic often called the "American Quadrant." Here Argentina, Chile and Great Britain have overlapping claims and, since the United States refuses to recognize *any* claims in the area, she has also become involved. The map on the following page indicates the extent and location of the area claimed by each country.

The fact that relatively little is known about this continent and the consequent need to make provisions for unpredictable contingencies go a long way toward explaining the keen competition for the acquisition of territory in such an uninviting place. The possibility of valuable resources, the effect of weather conditions, and strategic considerations of course figure in Argentine and Chilean interest. There is no certainty of any appreciable mineral deposits, but reports of the Chilean Ministry of Foreign Affairs have included a somewhat glowing picture of the possible resources along with the legal arguments advanced in support of their claim.[2]

Argentina and Chile are the most immediately affected by weather

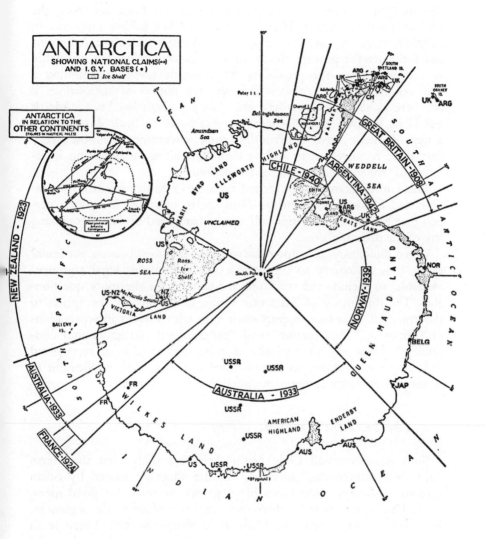

Source: Phillip C. Jessup and Howard J. Taubenfeld, *Controls for Outer Space and the Antarctic Analogy* (New York, 1959), insert, pp. 144–145; reproduced by permission of Columbia University Press.

patterns in the area and are understandably concerned over the need for weather observation installations and over any operation designed to change weather patterns.[3] The waters around the Antarctic are also thought to affect the waters and resources of the sea along the Chilean coast—a matter of real interest for her fishing industry. In addition, there are certain strategic considerations. Because Argentina and Chile are the powers closest to the Antarctic, they are justifiably apprehensive over the possibility of a hostile power establishing a base on the Palmer Peninsula. Finally, the impact of nationalism is felt here as almost everywhere else. Once a claim has been made, it would be political suicide for any government to back down. With a new domestic crisis confronting these governments almost every day, there is no reason to add to their difficulties by appearing indifferent to "the sovereign rights of the nation."

The United States is concerned because of future scientific operations and hemispheric security. Thus she is interested in making certain that her future activities will not be hampered by her recognizing any of the present claims.

When diplomacy calls upon international law to support a particular claim, it is customary to throw in every conceivable legal argument available, to include the well-founded along with the more questionable. The diplomacy of Antarctic claims is certainly no exception to this rule. All claimants support their title with various interpretations of "discovery," "occupation" and "geographical contiguity and continuity." These are all methods of territorial acquisition recognized as having some validity in international law. It is their application to specific circumstances that produces the controversy.

The bases for Antarctic claims

Both Argentina and Chile begin their case with what they term "historical antecedents," referring to title allegedly gained by Spain through discovery (sometimes papal grants are cited for good measure). The Spanish title by discovery was, according to the argument, inherited by Argentina and Chile after independence.[4] There is an initial difficulty here, however, because Chile claims the only valid title under the doctrine of *uti possidetis*, a doctrine which Argentina has chosen to invoke in other cases but finds inconvenient here.* The

* *Supra*, p. 130.

vague Spanish references to a "southern continent" or "lands in the southern seas" placed them under the jurisdiction of the Presidency of Chile. Thus Chile claims to be the sole rightful heir to Spain's "title." Quite naturally, Argentina prefers to skate lightly over this aspect and, more recently, her arguments have minimized the importance of discovery.[5]

But there is only questionable evidence that the Spanish were even certain of the existence of what we today know as the Antarctic. There were indeed vague references to a "southern continent" in Spanish decrees and some uncertain indications on early maps. But it is probable that these referred to a part of the South American continent (Tierra del Fuego) in some instances and were mere suppositions in others.[6] Although the British explorer Cook sailed around the Antarctic in 1774, there is very little evidence of any actual discovery of the continent itself until the nineteenth century.[7]

Even assuming the reality of Spanish discovery, however, it provides a hopelessly weak foundation for a claim. Before the end of the eighteenth century, international law required that discovery be followed by at least symbolic annexation. After this time the jurisprudence became more elaborate, eventually requiring that "effective occupation"[8] was essential for perfecting a title. The fact is that Spain did nothing to perfect this uncertain title (if indeed she even had it). What is more, neither Argentina nor Chile did anything to follow up so questionable an inheritance until nearly a century after they had gained their independence.[9]

Neither Argentina nor Chile rests its claim solely on discovery, however. Both argue that the inchoate title by discovery has been perfected by "effective occupation." But what constitutes "effective occupation"? There is certainly support in decisions of international tribunals for their contention that the requirement of "effective occupation" of so uninhabitable a place as the Antarctic can be satisfied by a very minimal type of "occupation." The classic statement on this was made by the Permanent Court of International Justice in the *Eastern Greenland* case.

It is impossible to read the records of the decisions in cases as to territorial sovereignty without observing that in many cases the tribunal has been satisfied with very little in the way of actual exercise of sovereign rights, provided that the other state could not make out a superior claim. This is particularly true in the case of claims to sovereignty over areas in thinly populated or unsettled countries.[10]

To say, however, that only minimal occupation gives Argentina or Chile a valid claim to *some* areas is quite different from saying that it supports the full extent of their present claims. Claims to enormous continental sectors are supported primarily on the basis of minimal activities on or around a few islands.

Chile's claim to effective occupation rests on certain administrative decrees, especially those regulating fishing in Antarctic waters.[11] But on closer examination we find that, until very recently, they applied only to *islands* and their surrounding waters, some of which were not even within the area now referred to as the "Antarctic." The report of the Chilean Ministry of Foreign Affairs for 1947 is particularly revealing on this point. After stating Chile's claim to the entire sector, and basing this upon "effective occupation," the report notes that up until this time it has not, unfortunately, been possible to send an official expedition to the Antarctic.[12] It was not until the following year that the first Chilean expedition was made.[13]

Argentine claims to have carried out "effective occupation" are equally tenuous. Such activities as are cited by that government have, until very recently, been confined to a few islands. Her first claim to the whole sector between 25° and 68° west longitude does not seem to have been made until 1942—but even that was nine years before her first expedition to the continent itself.[14]

After a very careful study of activities in the Antarctic area, these conclusions about Argentina and Chile were reached (and this refers only to activities in the islands, since continental activity came much later):

> Such is the outline of Argentina's activity. Laurie Island always excepted, there were no discoveries, nor formal annexations, and no display of state activities on the part of Argentina within the territories of the (Falkland Islands) Dependencies before the outbreak of the Second World War.[15]
> There was in fact no effective display of state activity by Chile until after the Second World War, no comment was made on the British Letters of Patent (1908, 1917) and it was not until 1939 that Chile, stimulated by Argentina and the United States' interest in the Antarctic, began seriously to consider its own position.[16]

British claims to have carried on activities which could be construed as "effective occupation" would seem to be at least as valid. Beginning in 1905, a series of administrative measures were applied to some of the islands (referred to as the Falkland Island Dependencies by Great Britain). Between 1912 and 1930, whaling regulations were enforced off the mainland (Graham Land), although from a base on Deception Island. Finally, between 1927 and 1939, "extensive surveys were made both of the South Shetlands and of Graham Land."[17]

Thus, before the World War II era, all Argentine and Chilean activity was confined to these scattered islands. On the basis of this, they claim about one-sixth of a continent the size of Europe and the United States combined. To make these claims more plausible they add arguments variously referred to as "contiguity," "continuity" and "the sector theory." These theories or "doctrines" are used to provide at least some sort of rationale for the assumption that activities carried out on some of the islands (hundreds of miles from the Antarctic mainland) implies "effective occupation," not only over the islands themselves but over large portions of the continent as well.

In the first place, the size of the continental area claimed bears no precise relationship to the location of the islands.[18] In both cases it extends to the east and to the west of them. This difficulty is bridged with the "sector theory," which quite arbitrarily divides the Antarctic into sectors and regards each sector as a geographical unit. International tribunals have in the past ruled that "effective occupation" in only parts of an area which forms a geographic unit is sufficient to establish title over the entire unit. But in the Argentine and Chilean view, by arbitrarily making their sectors a "geographic unit" the modest activities on islands would support claims to the mainland. The final aspect of the argument is that those states most contiguous to the various sectors should have a valid title over them by the very fact of their propinquity or contiguity.[19]

It has been argued that British title to a portion of the continent rests not on activities carried out on the several islands but on discovery and subsequent activities upon the mainland itself. A line drawn poleward from the extremes of these locations forms the British sector. Thus the British position is much more akin to the old hinterland doctrine than to the Argentine and Chilean sector claims.[20]

Although the United States has carried on the most extensive activities on the *mainland* of the Antarctic, it has thus far made no claims to sovereignty over any part of it. It has also refused to recognize anything but effective occupation as giving valid title and apparently does not regard any of the claimants as having achieved this. Thus it has recognized no claims to sovereignty in Antarctica.[21]

It should be pointed out, however, that as late as 1928 the United States, in support of other territorial claims, used some of the same arguments now proposed by Latin American states. In claiming sovereignty over a Pacific island disputed with the Netherlands, it was argued that Spanish title by discovery (three centuries earlier) had been inherited by the United States along with the Philippines.[22] Title was claimed on the basis of discovery which had been followed by *no* effective occupation whatever, and this only four years after Secretary of State Hughes' statement that we would recognize only "effective occupation" as a valid basis for title in Antarctica.[23]

No less a contrast was the basis for our claims over Oregon territories disputed with Great Britain in the mid-nineteenth century. Here we claimed title by original Spanish discovery which we had inherited through the Louisiana cession of 1803 and the Treaty of Florida Blanca in 1819 by which Spain had surrendered all her North American territory north of 42° north latitude. To this we added title by explorations of American citizens and, on the basis of a few trading posts on the Columbia River, claimed title to the whole river basin according to a convenient "watershed" criterion. "On both sides the evidence of acquisition by discovery and possession was vague and confused. All the 'visits' and 'explorations' had equally failed to be followed up either by effective settlement or by established agencies of control." [24] In an area more readily acceptable to "effective occupation" than the Antarctic, we were prepared to claim title by only the barest minimum of activity. The strength of the United States claim in this case was inversely proportional to the belligerency with which it was put forth by the expansionist Democratic administration of 1845–1849. War with Britain, however, could not be contemplated quite as casually as war with Mexico, and a compromise settlement was negotiated.[25]

Courts and conferences

In spite of all their legal arguments, Argentina and Chile have shown no inclination to have the existing Antarctic conflicts settled through judicial means. Both have turned down British offers (1954–1956) to submit their disputes to arbitration or to the International Court of Justice.[26] Chile has used the circular argument that, since this is manifestly Chilean territory, to bring such a controversy before an international tribunal would be to submit her national sovereignty to the judgment of third powers.[27] The Argentine argument, equally circular, insists that "the nation does not have to present any claim before any international tribunal in order to defend its rights."[28] Such arguments of course appeal to strong nationalistic feelings. Once they have been put in these emotional terms, they rule out any future impartial settlement.

In 1948, the United States, hoping to create some form of international regime for the Antarctic, proposed that a conference be convened among the eight states then most interested in the area. Only New Zealand and Great Britain were reported to be favorably inclined, and nothing came of the conference. In 1959, probably because of concern over renewed Soviet interest in the area, it was possible to convene a conference among the twelve states then engaged in Antarctic activities related to the International Geophysical Year.[29]

Both Argentina and Chile made it clear at the outset that they would have nothing to do with the creation of an international regime. In order to gain the cooperation of these two states, it was necessary to abandon the idea of a permanent solution to the question of sovereignty.[30] "Chile," said her Foreign Minister, "could only reject any proposal which might imply the internationalization of, or condominion over, any part of its National Territory, whether it be in Antarctica, in America, or in its insular possessions in the South Pacific."[31] The Argentine Foreign Minister announced that his country would "maintain its classic position retaining its rights over the Argentine claimed sector."[32]

Nevertheless, it was possible to conclude a treaty which should at least help facilitate future scientific activity. The most important feature of the treaty provided for a freezing of the *status quo* on all territorial claims. No acts or activities taking place while the treaty is in force will be regarded as a basis for asserting, supporting or denying territorial claims.[33] This was something of a concession on the part of the Great Powers, who are the most likely to be carrying on large-scale activities which might provide the basis for a claim. On the other hand, it did open the way for their scientific activities which might otherwise have been hampered by disputes over sovereignty.

Nuclear explosions and the dumping of radioactive wastes, matters of particular concern to Argentina and Chile, were banned from the area.[34] Full unilateral rights of inspection were accorded to each of the signatories. Each party to the treaty may designate nationals to serve as observers who will "have complete freedom of access at any time to any or all areas of Antarctica."[35]

A rather important concession was made by Argentina and Chile on the matter of jurisdiction over nationals. Both have national legislation which they claim applies to their Antarctic territories. Under the treaty, each party will have jurisdiction over its own nationals (scientists and observers only) in any part of Antarctica.[36]

An attempt to provide for compulsory adjudication of future disputes was defeated by the strong opposition of Argentina, Chile and the Soviet Union. The provision finally approved does no more than call upon the parties to avail themselves of the usual channels for peaceful settlement.[37]

Beyond the legal issues

The Antarctic offers no exception to the rule that states, as well as individuals, tend to support the law that best suits their situation. Here, as in other questions of law and politics, we find the small powers no less than the great powers willing to stretch the law to accommodate their national interests. Argentina has even resorted to the use of force in support of her claims. An Argentine-British-Chilean agreement to keep warships out of the area south of 60° south latitude (except for relief ships) was signed in 1948 and has been renewed each succeeding year. In spite of this, in 1952 the Argentine navy resorted to gunfire to force the withdrawal of a British meteorological party from the Hope Bay area.[38]

But, generally lacking power, Argentina and Chile have relied on other techniques to support their claims. One such technique is the appeal to what has appropriately been termed "underdeveloped area nationalism." It is a "nationalism" which goes beyond national borders and appeals to the common sentiments of other underdeveloped countries. In raising the specter of colonialism and imperialism, it makes a bid for the support of large areas of the world, regardless of the legal merits of the case.

No major power can for long thwart the nationalistic ambitions of these new (or newly assertive) states if the disputed matter of territory is deemed to lie within, or pertain to, the underdeveloped region. The Antarctic problem must be classified as such a dispute. After all the explanations and legal arguments are made, the Antarctic will still be regarded as land 'alien' to the British Isles. Chile and Argentina, regardless of the merits, can win the favor of world opinion. Students of world affairs have long recognized the strongest force in the world to be nationalism. In its modern form, the new nationalism of these underdeveloped countries is proving a formidable successor to its progenitor.[39]

Fully aware of this, Argentina and Chile have tried to make good, via inter-American politics, the defects that clearly exist in their legal titles to the Antarctic. Both Argentina and Chile brought this matter before the Ninth International Conference of American States as an issue of "anticolonialism." But efforts to remedy such defects have not been particularly successful. The resolutions approved by the conference only included Antarctica by implication—in the general references to "occupied territories."[40]

But neither country has made any really serious efforts to gain general American support. Both Argentina and Chile seem to have been content with making it clear that they regarded Antarctica as part of the whole question of colonialism in the Western Hemisphere. Chile did not even attend the meeting of the American Committee on Dependent Territories. Their rather mild efforts thus far do set certain precedents and at least indicate the general approach to be used should the question become more important in the future.

Now that the Soviet Union has shown an interest in the area, the anticolonial approach becomes less effective. As long as only Great Britain and the United States disputed the Argentine and Chilean claims, the charge of colonial domination might have had some effect. Both powers, under scrutiny and attack throughout uncommitted areas of the world, must now consider very carefully the impact of any forceful action they might take. The Soviet Union has not in the past shown undue concern for the charge of "imperialism" if it felt that a matter of genuine national interest was at stake. As long as neither the Soviet Union nor the United States was willing to support or even recognize *any* claims in the area, it is not easy to play one side against the other. Charging both powers with imperialism is not a particularly effective technique.

Hemispheric security considerations have also been used to emphasize the preferred position of American states, at least in the American Quadrant of the Antarctic. The Chilean delegate to the Washington Conference on Antarctica observed that "part of the American Antarctic is included within the 'continental security zone' created by the [Inter-American Treaty of Reciprocal Assistance] for which reason Chile considers that it would be advisable to state in the pertinent part that the provisions of the Antarctic Treaty in no way affect the principles contained in the aforementioned international instrument."[41] Establishment of the principle of preferred American rights in the area would at least strengthen the Argentine and Chilean position against

Britain, the state with the strongest legal case, and the U.S.S.R., potentially the most difficult contender. This would be especially true if the United States were willing to offer its support. Thus far it has shown no strong inclination in that direction, although it was willing to make a joint statement with the two Latin American countries following the Washington conference. Secretary of State Herter stated that, as far as Argentina, Chile and the United States were concerned, "the Antarctic Treaty does not affect their obligations under the Inter-American Treaty of Reciprocal Assistance."[42]

FOOTNOTES

1. This definition is used in the recent Antarctic Treaty, cited in footnote 33.
2. Chile, Ministerio de Relaciones Exteriores, *Memoria*, 1947, pp. 182–183.
3. Phillip C. Jessup and Howard J. Taubenfeld, *Controls for Outer Space and the Antarctic Analogy* (New York, 1959), pp. 163–164.
4. Chile, Ministerio de Relaciones Exteriores, *Memoria*, 1947, pp. 164–168; Robert D. Hayton, "The 'American' Antarctic," 50 *AJIL* (1956), p. 587.
5. In fact the Ministry of Foreign Affairs has observed that "Antarctica is the newest of all continents since knowledge of it dates from the year 1819. . . . Argentina has been the only country that has consistently maintained its representations in polar lands." Argentina, Ministerio de Relaciones Exteriores, Comisión Nacional del Antártico, *Las Islas Malvinas y el sector antártico argentino*, no pagination.
6. Jessup and Taubenfeld, *op. cit.*, p. 146; C. M. Waldock, "Disputed Sovereignty in the Falkland Island Dependencies," *British Year Book of International Law*, 1948, XXV, p. 326.
7. H. E. Archdale, "Claims to the Antarctic," *The Year Book of World Affairs*, 1958, pp. 250 ff.; Waldock, *op. cit.*, p. 319.
8. See *Island of Palmas* case, 22 *AJIL* (1928), pp. 735–752; L. F. Oppenheim, *International Law: A Treatise* (8th ed. by H. Lauterpacht, London, 1955), I, pp. 555 ff.
9. See Hayton, *op. cit.*, p. 351.
10. Permanent Court of International Justice, Series A/B, no. 53. See also the *Island of Palmas* case, cited, and the *Clipperton Island* case, 26 *AJIL* (1932), pp. 390 ff.
11. Oscar Pinochet-de la Barra, *Chilean Sovereignty in the Antarctic* (Santiago de Chile, n.d.), pp. 30 ff.; Chile, Ministerio de Relaciones Exteriores, *Memoria*, 1947, pp. 176 ff.
12. *Ibid.*, p. 179.
13. Pinochet-de la Barra, *op. cit.*, p. 55.
14. Argentina, Comisión Nacional del Antártico, *Antártida argentina* (Buenos Aires, 1949), pp. 44–47.
15. Waldock, *op. cit.*, p. 332.
16. *Ibid.*, p. 333.

17. *Ibid.*, pp. 327–328.
18. *Ibid.*, p. 346; Hayton, *op. cit.*, pp. 605 ff.
19. Chile, Ministerio de Relaciones Exteriores, *Memoria*, 1947, pp. 168–171; Hayton, *op. cit.*, pp. 604 ff. Another related aspect of the Chilean claim is that the Antarctic is an extension of the American continent.
20. Waldock, *op. cit.*, pp. 340–341.
21. Phillip C. Jessup, "International Law at World's End and Beyond," *Columbia University Forum*, III (Winter, 1960), p. 16.
22. 22 *AJIL* (1928), pp. 735–741.
23. G. H. Hackworth, *Digest*, I, pp. 449–465.
24. Corbett, *Law and Society in the Relations of States* (New York, 1951), p. 107.
25. *Ibid.*, pp. 107–108.
26. ICJ *Pleadings, Antarctic Case* (United Kingdom v. Argentina; United Kingdom v. Chile), pp. 35–36, 73, 90–97.
27. Hayton, *op. cit.*, p. 593.
28. Argentina, Ministerio de Relaciones Exteriores, *Las Islas Malvinas y el sector antártico argentino*, no pagination.
29. Howard J. Taubenfeld, "A Treaty for Antarctica," *International Conciliation* (January 1961), pp. 277, 280–281.
30. *Ibid.*, p. 280.
31. *Ibid.*, pp. 278–279.
32. *Ibid.*, p. 279.
33. Article IV, *The Antarctic Treaty*, signed December 1, 1959, reproduced *ibid.*, pp. 318–322.
34. Article V.
35. Article VII.
36. Article VIII.
37. Article XI.
38. Jessup and Taubenfeld, *op. cit.*, p. 149.
39. Hayton, *op. cit.*, p. 608.
40. International Conference of American States, Ninth, *Actas y documentos*, II, pp. 263 ff.
41. U.S. Department of State, *The Conference on the Antarctic*, publication 7060 (Washington, D.C., 1960), p. 18.
42. U.S. Department of State, *Bulletin*, 41 (1959), p. 483.

Chapter Nine

Patterns of Law and Politics

Law and politics are inseparable. The vital issues in inter-American diplomacy cannot be analyzed intelligently without an understanding of the legal doctrines and arguments which are injected. It is easy enough to dismiss these doctrines as diplomatic double-talk, but the complex and powerful forces which condition them tell us they will not go away that easily. Some of the broad patterns of law and politics that emerge from our analyses provide a framework for the study of inter-American diplomacy.

Latin America is in a period of profound revolutionary change. Economic and social structures which have remained virtually unchanged for centuries are now undergoing radical transformations. In other instances, significant but less obvious changes—such as the emergence of middle sectors in the social-economic structure—which have been developing for a long time, have only recently begun to make their impact felt. These revolutionary changes within national societies have a profound impact not only on domestic law but on international law as well. During all such periods, law is usually ineffective both within nations and among them. "Law by its very nature, conserves the values of a going social system. And when the values are themselves in transition, the system of law gives way to political or quasi-legal activity."[1]

Thus the changes within Latin American societies have spilled over into the international politics of the Western Hemisphere and are having a significant impact on legal norms once claimed as binding.

For example, movements for economic and social reform are felt in the growing resentment against remaining dictators who symbolize old oligarchic orders. This resentment has led to action across national borders and to a variety of doctrines about new interpretations of the old rule on non-intervention. Quasi-legal instruments in the form of declarations and resolutions against communism, dictatorship and social injustice become more and more precise at the very time that declarations and resolutions against intervention become stronger and more comprehensive. The traditional Latin American position on recognition of governments, which held that governments exercising *de facto* control and able to discharge international obligations ought to be recognized, has been rejected or questioned in many parts of the hemisphere. Attempts to deal with intervention and recognition on a collective basis become tangled in the same web of social revolution and cold war. Much of inter-American diplomacy is now concerned with reconciling this dilemma.

These revolutionary conditions are also reflected in a growing demand for recognition of changes in the very structure of international society. It is felt that many of the most important norms in international law were developed and perpetuated by a few Western European powers and the United States, all of whom shared a large community of interests, and that these rules were often forced on much of the rest of the world. The Latin American states, who have in many respects remained "colonial" societies, have found themselves at odds with many of the traditional norms. In the controversies over territorial waters, Antarctica and European colonial possessions, this attitude is especially evident. The rules that reduced the breadth of territorial waters to a minimum are regarded as serving the interests of states with large merchant marines, navies and fishing fleets. The European rights to colonial possessions here are seen to be based on rules which recognized the validity of the use of force—the means by which they have perpetuated control over disputed territories. These would be replaced by rules based on certain principles declared valid by the American states—the preferred maritime rights of coastal states and the illegality of colonial domination. The rules relating to the treatment of aliens and their property reflect this same attitude—the traditional rules are held to reflect the interests of states with large financial investments abroad.

These attitudes have, of course, existed for a long time in Latin America. But they find increased expression and application with the new elites which are emerging. The very social pressures which are

producing these new elites "require" that the latter change many of
the previously accepted rules governing the relations between states.
For example, the old military-oligarchic elites were usually quite as
content in maintaining the traditional rules on compensation for expropriated private property as were the elites in capital-investing
countries. But new elites, whose position in power requires that they
bring about sweeping changes in the economic and social order, often
take quite a different point of view. In fact their position in power
may even require that the power of economic interests be broken by
outright confiscation. The older elites are now pictured as having
engaged in a conspiracy with the large foreign economic interests.

The relationship between law and politics in the Western Hemisphere has been much influenced by the long-time existence of inter-
American "organizations." To say that they have provided a forum
for inter-American discussions by no means tells the whole story. Just
as the United Nations was for a time largely a United States–led alliance against the U.S.S.R., the inter-American conferences have often
had all the earmarks of a Latin American alliance against the United
States. The United States has generally been able to use its influence
with enough governments to prevent the "alliance" from including
all or even a majority of Latin American states. But when Latin Americans have been able to agree on certain principles or norms which
they wished to establish as binding, they have been able to make this
united position publicly known. This at least has given their position
more weight than it would have had in individual diplomatic exchanges. It should be emphasized also that inter-American conferences
receive far more publicity, even in the popular press, in Latin America than in the United States. Thus they become a factor in the formation of public opinion and popular support.

One of the chief functions of the inter-American system, in the eyes
of the United States, has been that of marshaling Latin American support when some threat was presented from the outside. Although the
United States has often faced initial difficulties, its overwhelming
power and influence has nearly always guaranteed success for its resolutions or declarations on "American principles." Latin American
states too have increasingly turned to the technique of offering a resolution or declaration on some "American principle" which would support them in specific conflicts with extracontinental powers. But more
often than not they find it impossible to gain the indispensable support of the United States, either because the latter shares the particular
interest of the extracontinental powers or because it would be politi-

cally unwise to oppose them. Given the worldwide scope of United States interests and commitments, there is reason to believe that this problem will become increasingly complicated.

Finally, some signs of "horse trading" and bargaining, basic elements in reaching effective norms in national societies, are beginning to emerge in rudimentary form. For example, United States attempts to gain legal sanction for desired action against Communist infiltration have been met with attempts to tie this issue with economic under-development and the existence of dictatorship. In view of the Latin American reaction to the procedures of Mr. Dulles at Caracas (in pushing through his resolution on Guatemala while showing a notable lack of interest in economic and social issues which concerned most Latin Americans), quite a different approach was used at San José. It was no coincidence that the United States supported the anti-Trujillo resolution and came to the conference with an offer of $600,000,000 in economic assistance in the hope of getting support for an anti-Castro resolution.

The competition between the United States and the Soviet Union has become an important factor in the relationship between law and politics in the Western Hemisphere. Out of this competition have come two conflicting tendencies in the Latin American policy of the United States. On the one hand, United States concern for its security has forced it to accept, *de facto*, if not *de jure*, certain changes in ac-cepted norms of international conduct as a concession to the mainte-nance of satisfactory relations with its southern neighbors. It is real-ized that arbitrary action on the part of the United States helps to strengthen the growing anti-Yankee sentiment throughout the hemi-sphere. Although there has not in the past been serious concern that these nations would join the Soviet bloc, there has always been the possibility that they would move closer to the periphery of the United States bloc and even into the neutralist group. The Guate-malan and Cuban affairs have convinced United States policy makers that there is now a serious danger of Latin American states moving into the Soviet bloc.

A similar situation had been presented with the Fascist threat begin-ning in the 1930's. Then, recognizing the importance of improving its relations with the Latin American countries, the United States reversed its long-standing but unpopular position on the right of mili-tary intervention to protect the property and interests of its citizens. The same situation brought the United States to accept a compromise settlement on property that had been expropriated by Mexico. More recently, extensive Latin American claims over territorial waters, reinforced by concrete action against United States fishing interests, have called up only verbal protests.

Paradoxically, the bipolar power struggle may also bring the United States to disregard certain so-called "American principles" if the immediate issue is of sufficient importance. Our recent action with regard to Cuba is an indication of this and was only emphasized by President Kennedy's warning that "if the nations of this hemisphere should fail to meet their commitments against outside communist penetration . . . this Government will not hesitate in meeting its primary obligations." But action of this sort serves only to cut even more deeply the channels of another pattern in inter-American law and politics. In so doing, it makes the growth of an inter-American legal order just that much more difficult.

This pattern bears the imprint of the dominant theme in Latin American efforts to form a regional legal order. These efforts contain a real paradox, for they set a course which inevitably aims at the very antithesis of the legal order so ardently embraced. The paradox was evident in almost every discussion and speech presented at Havana in 1928. The Latin American conception of an inter-American legal order has shown (and not without reason) an obsession with the principle of the sovereignty and independence of individual states. This obsession found expression in nearly all the projects presented to the Havana conference. James Brierly's remarkably perceptive criticism of these projects likened them to a "Declaration of Independence."[2] "But," he noted, "there is no super national tyrant in being or in prospect today against whom these fulminations can fitly be directed. . . . The battle-cry that we need is not one that proclaims 'the complete independence, liberty, and sovereignty' of every state, but one that will teach the need of national sacrifice, and that note is hardly to be heard at all in these projects."

There may not have been any "super national tyrant," as Brierly observed, but many Latin Americans had a "tyrant" in mind. That "tyrant" was none other than the United States. Many Boston Irish are not at all certain that George III is dead: many more Latin Americans are not at all convinced that the tyrant of dollar diplomacy is dead. The Irish doubts may be a litttle difficult to understand, but the Latin American doubts cannot be brushed aside so easily. Be that as it may, the emphasis on sovereignty and independence has been the dominant theme at each of the subsequent inter-American conferences. To be sure, each of these conferences has added something to the building of an inter-American legal order. But that "something" continues to struggle against the antithetical theme of sovereignty and independence. This theme reflects more than the desire to preserve freedom of action. It is the reflection of a very real fear that inter-American institutions and machinery will become the vehicle for United States domination. Widespread Latin American support for institutions or arrangements for ordering various aspects of inter-American relations inevitably become snagged in this touchy problem.

Although it is perhaps too early to determine the impact of the Kennedy statement on this climate of opinion, there can be no doubt that many thoughtful Latin Americans must have interpreted it as did one very competent scholar in the United States.

The real meaning of the Kennedy statement is the affirmation of the supremacy of national interests and spheres of influence over the moral and legal restraints imposed by international law. This may be the result of a grim appraisal of the rapidly worsening international situation, and admission that only force, strategy and logistics can henceforth count in the struggle between the great power blocs. It may mean that America, no more than Russia or China, will tolerate in its own sphere of power a type of government that it distrusts. But the implications of such a doctrine should be realized.[3]

In order to realize these implications we might do worse than to call upon the counsel of the very statesman whose name has become synonymous with *real politik*—Niccolò Machiavelli. He did indeed advise the Prince to resort to force and fraud where necessary. But he also saw the long-term implications of this kind of policy. Thus he advised the Prince that he would do well to commit all his arbitrary acts at once and be through with them. "*Whoever acts otherwise, either through timidity or bad counsel, is always obliged to stand with knife in hand, and can never depend on his subjects, because they, owing to continually fresh injuries, are unable to depend upon him.*" If Machiavelli knew how all these arbitrary acts could be committed at once and then dispensed with, he did not impart this particular bit of wisdom to us. Indeed, Machiavelli's "Prince" (Cesare Borgia) seems to have found it necessary to "stand with knife in hand," and he came to a rather ignoble end.

The hemisphere which has talked so much about ordering its affairs according to generally accepted rules of conduct now stands at a crucial juncture. It may be that today's social revolutions and the legacies of colonialism and imperialism will make it impossible to find

162 LAW AND POLITICS IN INTER-AMERICAN DIPLOMACY

mutually acceptable rules. It may be that cold war "requirements" presage a new and grimmer phase in United States policy, which will abandon efforts to secure the rule of law in international affairs. The foregoing analysis has assessed today's battered "rules" in the light of the requirements of a hemisphere already quite different from the "world community" in which those rules emerged. If it has pointed out the general directions for serious and more detailed study of the substance of rules which might hope to bring or preserve a measure of order and stability in inter-American relations, it has accomplished its purpose.

FOOTNOTES

1. Morton A. Kaplan and Nicholas deB. Kazenbach, "Patterns of International Politics and of International Law," *American Political Science Review*, LIII (1959), pp. 703–704.
2. In Hersch Lauterpacht, ed., *The Basis of Obligation in International Law and Other Papers by the Late James Leslie Brierly* (Oxford, 1958), pp. 121 ff. The paper is a reprint from the *British Yearbook of International Law*, 1926.
3. From a "Letter to the Editor" of *The New York Times*, by W. Friedmann, *New York Times*, May 1, 1961.

Index

Alliance for Progress: 84

American Committee on Dependent Territories, Havana Meeting (1949): 137–138

American Institute of International Law: projects proposed for law of recognition in the Hemisphere, 12–13

American Revolution: 7

Anti-Smuggling Act of 1935: 107

Arévalo, Juan José: elected president of Guatemala, 17; leads Guatemala in breaking relations with the Dominican Republic, 17–18

Argentina: presidency of Hipólito Irigoyen, 16; Farrell Administration, 21; intervention in South America, 67–68; at Tenth International Conference, 75; claims to territorial waters, 112; claims to the Falkland Islands, 126, 128ff., 148–149; opposition to proposed declaration of the Seventh Meeting of Foreign Ministers at San José, 127–128; claims to territory in the Antarctic, 145ff.

Balance of power: 7

Batista, Fulgencio: overthrow by Castro forces in 1959, 20

Betancourt, Rómulo: installed provisional president of Venezuela, 18; attitudes on Trujillo regime, 19; threatened assassination of, 26

Bogotá Conference (Ninth International Conference, 1948): 1; recognition controversy at, 23–25; discussion of concept of non-intervention, 51; pressures for the establishment of an Inter-American Court, 52

Bolivia: Revolution of May, 1936, 14–15; expropriation of Standard Oil holdings, 15; Argentine intervention in, 67–68; asylum during 1946 revolution, 94; expropriation of Patiño tin interests, 44–45; M.N.R., 1948–1952, 19

Brazil: views on Hemispheric aggression, 81; claims to territorial waters, 112

Buenos Aires Conference (Inter-American Conference for the Maintenance of Peace, 1936): discussion of non-intervention at, 50; resolution on intervention, 80; proposal of Inter-American Court, 52

Byrnes, James F.: 22

Canning, George: 8

Expropriation: 55–57; problem basic to present Hemispheric recognition policies, 26; Mexican case involving U.S. oil holdings, 38–42; Guatemalan case involving properties of United Fruit Co., 42–44; Bolivian case involving the Patiño tin interests, 44–45

Florida Blanca, Treaty of: 150
Foreign ministers, meetings of: 4; first (Panama City, 1939), 108, 119; second (Havana, 1940), 127; third (Rio, 1942), 21; fifth (Santiago, 1959), 67, 76–78; sixth (San José, 1960), 25–26; seventh (San José, 1960), 78
French Revolution: 7

García Amador, F. V.: views on exploration of submarine areas, 120–121
Geneva Conference on Fishing and Conservation of Living Resources of the High Seas: 115
Geneva Conference on the Law of the Sea (1958): 111–112, 115; U.S. position on the territorial sea question, 119–120
Geneva Conference on the Law of the Sea (1960): 116
German Federal Republic: views on the territorial sea, 120
Good Neighbor Policy: 14
Great Britain: early practice in recognition of governments, 8; views on the Antarctic regions, 151
Guatemala: overthrow of the Ubico regime, 17; administration of Juan José Arévalo, 17; breaks relations with the Dominican Republic, 17–18; project on recognition at Mexico City Conference (1945), 17–18, 23–24; expropriation of United Fruit holdings in 1953, 42–44; discussed at the Caracas Conference, 73–75; claims to territorial waters, 112; claims to British Honduras (Belice), 126, 128, 130ff., 148–149

Hague Conference (second): partial recognition of Drago Doctrine, 48

Haiti: 91, 92–93; complaints against Caribbean intervention, 72
Harding, Warren G.: 11–12
Havana Conference (Sixth International Conference, 1928): important projects submitted to, 4; recognition of governments discussed at, 13; discussion of problem of intervention, 48–49, 65, 76–77, 160
Herter, Christian: 154
Holy Alliance: 7
Hoover, Herbert: on intervention in the Hemisphere, 14
Hughes, Charles E.: at Havana Conference, 48–49
Hull, Cordell: views on intervention, 14, 109

Inter-American Council of Jurists: 5; role in recognition controversy after Bogotá Conference, 24–25; asked to prepare report on state responsibility, 51; 1950 views on territorial waters, 112–113; 1956 position on territorial waters, 114
Inter-American Juridical Committee: 5, 54, 77, 99–100
Inter-American Peace Committee: 77
Inter-American Treaty of Reciprocal Assistance: 72, 153–154
International Commission of Jurists: created, 4; 1927 meeting, 12
International geophysical year (1959): 151
International Law Commission, Seventh Session (1955): 115–116
Irigoyen, Hipólito: elected president of Argentina, 1916, 16

Jefferson, Thomas: 8, 106

Legitimacy, doctrine of: 7

Maúrtua, Dr. Victor: at Havana Conference (1928), 49–50, 52
Mexican Revolution: 2
Mexico City Conference (Second International Conference, 1901–1902): 4